1000 FACTS ON

BUILDINGS &
TRANSPORTATION

First published in 2002 by Miles Kelly Publishing Ltd
Bardfield Centre, Great Bardfield
Essex, U.K., CM7 4SL

This edition published by Barnes & Noble, Inc.

2 4 6 8 10 9 7 5 3 1

Editor
Isla MacCuish

Design
WhiteLight

Picture Research
Liberty Newton

Americanization
Cindy Leaney

Library of Congress Cataloging-in-Publication Data on file at the Library of Congress.

2004 Barnes & Noble Books

ISBN 0-7607-5391-1

Printed and bound in China

1000 FACTS ON
BUILDINGS &
TRANSPORTATION

John Farndon
Consultant Brian Williams

BARNES
&NOBLE
BOOKS
NEW YORK

Contents

Key

Cars

Trains

Planes

Buildings

Great Monuments

Boats

Contents

Contents

The Benz

- **Karl Benz (1844–1929)** and his wife Berta were the German creators of the first successful gasoline-powered car in 1885.

- **At the age of 16** before Lenoir built his gasoline-powered cart, Karl Benz dreamed of "a unit that could supplant the steam engine."

- **Karl and Berta Benz** began developing their car in the 1870s, while trying to earn money from a tin-making business. By 1880, they were so penniless they could barely afford to eat every day.

▼ *The Benz tricycle was the world's first successful gasoline-powered car.*

- **Their first car** was a small tricycle, but it had a water-cooled four-stroke engine with electric ignition.

- **Karl Benz** tested the car around the streets of their home town of Mannheim after dark to avoid scaring people.

- **Berta Benz** recharged the car's battery after each trip by pedaling a dynamo attached to her sewing machine.

▲ *A Benz automobile from 1925.*

- **Berta Benz** made the first long, 60 mi (100 km) journey in the car, without Karl knowing. On the journey to her home in Pforzheim, she had to clear the fuel line with a hairpin and use her garters to cure an electrical short.

- **The Benz** caused a stir when shown at the Paris World Fair in 1889.

- **Backed by F. von Fischer** and Julian Ganss, Benz began making his cars for sale in 1889—the first cars ever made for sale.

- **By 1900** Benz was making over 600 cars a year.

Model T Ford

◀ *Ford cars are still among the most popular on sale today.*

● **In 1905** most cars were "coach-built" which meant they were individually built by hand. This made them costly toys available only to the rich.

● **The dream of Detroit farmboy** Henry Ford was to make "a motor car for the great multitude—a car so low in price that no man making a good fortune will be unable to own one."

● **Ford's solution** was to make a car, which he called the Model T, using a mass-production technique.

● **Mass production** meant using huge teams of men, each adding a small part to the car as it moved along the production line.

● **Body-panels** for the Model T were stamped out by machines, not hammered by hand as with earlier cars.

● **In 1908** when Ford launched the Model T, fewer than 200,000 people in the U.S.A. owned cars.

● **In 1913** 250,000 people owned Model Ts alone.

● **By 1930** 15 million Model Ts had been sold.

- **One of the keys to the T** was standardizations. Ford said early Ts were available in "any color they like so long as it's black." Later models came in other colors.

- **The T's fragile-looking chassis** earned it the nickname "Tin Lizzie," but it was made of tough vanadium steel.

▲ *The tough, cheap, and reliable Model T—the first mass-produced car—put America on the road for the first time and earned the affection of two generations of American families.*

Early cars

- **In 1890** Frenchman Emile Levassor made the first real car, with an engine at the front. He laughed, saying, "C'est brutal, mais ca marche" ("It's rough, but it goes").

- **The Duryea** brothers made the first successful American car in 1893.

- **Early accidents** made cars seem dangerous. Until 1896 in Britain and 1901 in New York, cars had to be preceded by a man on foot waving a red flag.

- **In 1895** the French Panhard-Levassor company made the first covered "saloon" car.

- **In 1898** Renault drove the wheels with a shaft not a chain.

- **The Oldsmobile Curved Dash** of 1900 was the first car to sell in thousands.

- **On early cars** speed was controlled by moving a small ignition advance lever backward or forward.

▼ *Frederick Lanchester designed some of the world's earliest motor cars. He built his first automobile in 1896.*

▲ *By 1904, many cars were starting to have the familiar layout of cars today—engine at the front, driver on one side, steering wheel, gas tank at the back, a shaft to drive the wheels, and so on.*

- **Dirt roads**, oil spray, and noise meant early motorists needed protective clothing such as goggles.

- **The first cars** had wooden or wire-spoked wheels. Pressed-steel wheels like today's came in after 1945.

- **In 1906** an American steam-driven car, the Stanley Steamer, broke the Land Speed Record at over 127 mph (205 km/h).

Luxury cars

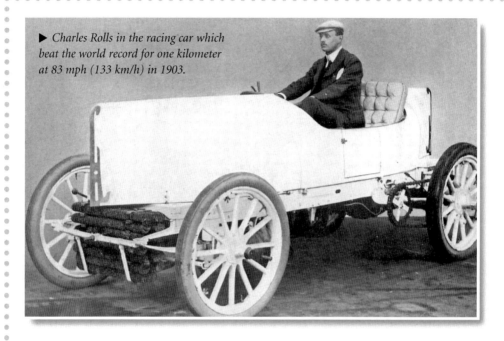

▶ *Charles Rolls in the racing car which beat the world record for one kilometer at 83 mph (133 km/h) in 1903.*

- **The first Rolls-Royce** was made by Charles Rolls and Henry Royce. It was known as the "best car in the world."

- **The Rolls-Royce Silver Ghost** got its name for its ghost-like quietness and shiny aluminum body.

- **Today** each Rolls-Royce takes three months to build.

- **The winged girl** statuette on the hood of a Rolls-Royce is called "Spirit of Ecstasy" and dates from 1911.

- **In the 1930s** Ettore Bugatti set out to build the best car ever with the Bugatti Royale. Only six were built, and they are now the world's most valuable cars.

- **The name Royale** comes from the King of Spain, Alfonso XIII, who was to buy the first model.

- **In 1925,** drinks-maker André Dubonnet had a special version of the Hispano-Suiza H6B built with a body made entirely of tulipwood.

- **In the 1930s** American car-makers like Cord, Auburn, and Packard made magnificent cars that Hollywood stars posed beside and Chicago gangsters drove.

- **Every 1934** Auburn speedster sold had a plaque certifying it had been driven at over 100 mph (160 km/h) by racing driver Ab Jenkins.

- **The Mercedes in** Mercedes-Benz was the name of the daughter of Emil Jellinek, who sold the cars in the U.S.A.

▶ *Bentley is one of the great names in luxury cars. But founder Owen Bentley believed in racing as advertisement. The Bentley name gained lasting fame with success in the Le Mans 24-hour races of the 1920s. This is a 1950s rally entry.*

15

People's cars

▲ *The 1959 Mini, designed by Alec Issigonis, set a trend in small-car design, with the engine mounted across the car driving the front wheels.*

- **The first car** for ordinary people was Ford's Model T. Ford built their ten millionth car in 1924 and their 50 millionth in 1959.

- **The U.S.A.** began making more than a million cars a year in 1916, of which over a third were Model Ts. No other country made a million cars a year until the U.K. in 1954.

- **Ford U.S.** introduced weekly installment plans for new cars in 1923. The Nazis later borrowed the idea for the VW Beetle.

- **The Model A Ford** sold a million within 14 months of its launch in December 1927. The Ford Escort of 1980 sold a million in just 11 months.

- **The French Citroën 2CV** was designed to carry "a farmer in a top hat across a plowed field without breaking the eggs on the seat beside him."

- **The VW Beetle** was the brainchild of the Nazi dictator Adolf Hitler who wanted a cheap car to be available for all Germans. It was created in 1938 by Ferdinand Porsche.

- **The war interrupted** VW Beetle production when it had barely begun, but it was resumed after the war.

- **The ten millionth** VW Beetle was built in 1965. Over 22 million have now been sold.

- **The Soviet-built Lada**, based on a design by Fiat, was one of the most inexpensive cars ever.

- **The first British car** to sell a million was the Morris Minor, between 1949 and 1962.

▲ *The German Volkswagen Beetle was first driven in 1938. A new-look design came out in 1998.*

Supercars

◀ *The Porsche 911 is one of the classic supercars, first introduced in 1964, but still looking sleek many years later.*

- **The Mercedes Benz 300SL** of 1952 was one of the first supercars of the post-war years, famous for its stylish flip-up "Gullwing" doors.

- **The Jaguar E-type** was the star car of the early 1960s with incredibly sleek lines and 155 mph (250 km/h) performance.

- **The Ford Mustang** was one of the first young and lively "pony" cars, introduced in 1964.

- **The Aston Martin DB6** was the classic supercar of the late 1960s, driven by film spy James Bond.

- **The Porsche 911 turbo** was the fastest accelerating production car for almost 20 years after its launch in 1975, scorching from 0 to 60 mph (100 km/h) in just 5.4 seconds.

- **The Lamborghini** Countach was the fastest supercar of the 1970s and 1980s, with a top speed of 183 mph (295 km/h).

- **The McLaren F1** can accelerate from 0 to 100 mph (160 km/h) in less time than it takes to read this sentence.

- **The McLaren F1** is capable of going from 0 to 100 mph (160 km/h) and back to 0 again in under 20 seconds.

- **A tuned version** of the Chevrolet Corvette, the Callaway Sledge Hammer, can hit over 250 mph (400 km/h).

> **FASCINATING FACT**
> The Ford GT-90 zooms from 0 to 60 mph (0 to 100 km/h) in 3.2 seconds.

▲ *Mercedes wins the Fomula One World Championship in 1954.*

Record-breaking cars

Tiny windshield providing driver's only view

Bristol-Siddeley Proteus 705 gas-turbine engine pushing out 4500 horsepower

Tail-plane for stability

Drive shaft

Differential gear

Air intake

Gas cylinders

Driver's cockpit

Lightweight aluminum wheels

Total weight of car is 9,600 lb (4,354 kg)

Exhaust ducts

Solid rubber tires

Streamlined body shell for minimum drag

...FASCINATING FACT...
On October 13, 1997, a British jet car called *Thrust SSC* driven by British fighter pilot Andy Green broke the sound barrier for the first time. In two runs across Nevada's Black Rock desert it hit over 758 mph (1,220 km/h).

▲ *Donald Campbell took on the record-breaking mantle of his father, and the Bluebird name for his car. On July 17, 1964, Campbell's Bluebird hit a world record 429.3 mph (690.909 km/h) on the salt flats at Lake Eyre in South Australia. At one moment he hit over 445 mph (716 km/h), faster than any wheel-driven car has ever been.*

- **The first car speed record** was achieved by an electric Jentaud car in 1898 at Acheres near Paris. Driven by the Comte de Chasseloup-Laubat, the car hit 39.2 mph (63.14 km/h.)

- **Daytona Beach** in Florida became a venue for speed trials in 1903.

- **The biggest engine** ever to be raced in a Grand Prix was the 19,891 cc V4 of American Walter Christie, which he entered in the 1907 French Grand Prix. Later the Christie was the first front-wheel-drive car to win a major race—a 250 mi (400 km) race on Daytona Beach.

- **The record** for the circuit at Brooklands, England was set in 1935 by John Cobb in a Napier-Railton at 1 min 0.41 sec (143.4 mph/230.79 km/h) and never beaten.

- **In 1911** the governing body for the Land Speed Record said that cars had to make two runs in opposite directions over a 0.6 mi (1 km) course to get the record.

- **In 1924** Sir Malcolm Campbell broke the Land Speed Record for the first of many times in a Sunbeam at 146 mph (235.17 km/h.) In 1925 he hit 150 mph (242 km/h) for the first time. But his most famous record-breaking runs were in the 1930s in his own *Bluebird* cars.

- **In 1947** John Cobb drove with tremendous skill to reach 394 mph (634.27 km/h) in his Railton-Mobil. This stood as the record for 17 years.

- **In 1964** the rules were changed to allow jet and rocket-propelled cars to challenge for the Land Speed Record. The next year Craig Breedlove drove his three-wheeler jet *Spirit of America* to over 500 mph (846.78 km/h.)

- **In 1970** Gary Gabelich set the record over 621 mph (1000 km/h) in his rocket-powered *Blue Flame*. This record wasn't beaten until Richard Noble roared to 633 mph (1019.37 km/h) in his jet-powered *Thrust 2* in 1983.

Gears

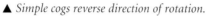

▲ *Simple cogs reverse direction of rotation.*

▲ *Rack and pinion changes rotation to sliding motion.*

▼ *Bevels move direction of rotation through a right angle.*

▼ *Worm gears turn fast rotation into slower, stronger rotation at right angles.*

▶ *Gears are used in a huge range of machines, from watches to motorcycles, for transmitting movement from one shaft to another.*

- **Gears** are pairs of toothed wheels that interlock and so transmit power from one shaft to another.

- **The first gears** were wooden, with wooden teeth. By the 6th century AD, wooden gears of all kinds were used in windmills, watermills, and winches.

- **Metal gears** appeared in 87BC and were later used for clocks. Today, all gears are metal and made on a "gear-hobbing" machine.

- **Simple gears** are wheels with straight-cut teeth.

- **Helical gears** have slanting rather than straight teeth, and run smoother. The gears in cars are helical.

- **Bevel or miter gears** are cone-shaped, allowing the gear shafts to interlock at right angles.

- **In worm gears** one big helical gear interlocks with a long spiral gear on a shaft at right angles.

- **Planetary gears** have a number of gear wheels known as spurs or planets that rotate around a central "sun" gear.

- **In a planetary gear** the planet and sun gear all rotate within a ring called an annulus.

> ....**FASCINATING FACT**....
> Automatic gearboxes in cars use
> planetary or epicyclic gears.

Bicycles

▲ *Bicycles are the cheapest, most reliable form of transportation ever, and in the 1920s many tradesmen adapted them for use.*

- **The first bicycle** was the 1818 "draisienne" of Baron de Drais. The rider scooted his feet on the ground to move.

- **In 1839** Scots blacksmith Kirkpatrick Macmillan invented the first bicycle with pedals and brakes.

- **On Macmillan's velocipede** pedals were linked by rods to cranks on the back wheel. These turned the wheel slowly.

- **In 1861** French father and son Pierre and Ernest Michaux stuck the pedals directly on the front wheel to make the first successful bicycle, nicknamed "boneshaker."

- **In 1870** James Starley improved the boneshaker with the Ordinary. A huge front wheel gave high speed with little pedaling.

- **In 1874** H. J. Lawson made the first chain-driven bicycle. This was called a "safety bicycle" because it was safer than the tall Ordinary.

- **In 1885** Starley's nephew John made the Rover Safety bicycle. Air-filled tires were added in 1890, and the modern bicycle was born.

- **By 1895** four million Americans were riding bicycles.

- **Today** 50 million people in the U.S.A. cycle regularly.

- **More people** in China cycle today than in the rest of the world put together.

▼ *Bicycle-riding has grown in popularity and many cities have established special lanes for cyclists in parks and along streets.*

Motorcycles

- **The first gasoline engine** motorcycle was built by Gottlieb Daimler in Germany in 1885.

- **Most small motorcycles** have a two-stroke gasoline engine, typically air-cooled and quite noisy.

- **Most larger motorcycles** have four-stroke gasoline engines, which typically are water-cooled.

- **On most motorcycles** the engine drives the rear wheel through a chain; on some the drive is through a shaft.

- **A trail bike** is a bike with a high mounted frame and chunky tires, designed to be ridden over rough tracks.

- **In Britain, motorcycles** with engines smaller than 50cc may be called mopeds, because in the past they had pedals as well as an engine.

◄ *Many enthusiasts still ride motorbikes like this from the 1930s when motorcycling was in its heyday.*

26

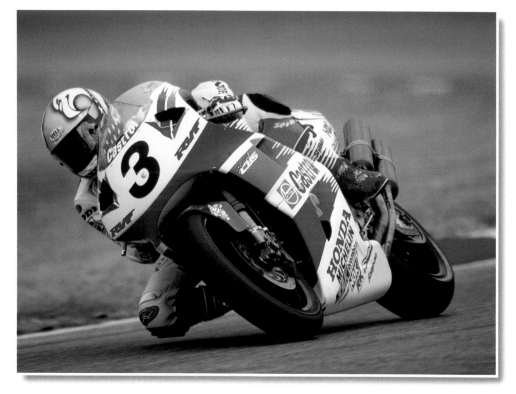

▲ *The rider of a superbike crouches as low as possible over the handlebars to minimize wind resistance.*

- **The biggest motorcycles** have engines of around 1200cc.

- **The most famous** motorcycle race in the world is the Isle of Man TT, or Tourist Trophy.

- **In Speedway,** motorcycles with no brakes or gears are raced on dirt tracks.

Trucks

- **Trucks** can weigh 40 tons or more—maybe as much as 50 automobiles.

- **Cars** or automobiles are normally powered by gasoline engines; trucks are typically powered by diesel engines.

- **Cars** typically have five forward gears; trucks often have as many as 16.

- **Cars** typically have four wheels. Trucks often have 12 or 16 to help spread the weight of the loads they need to carry.

- **Many trucks** have the same basic cab and chassis (the framework supporting the body). Different bodies are fitted on to the chassis to suit the load.

 ▲ *Huge trucks transport heavy machinery used for farming and building.*

▲ *Many trucks are fitted with refrigeration sytems. This means they can carry huge loads of perishable goods, such as food, over long distances.*

- **Some trucks** are constructed in two parts, hinged at the join. These are called trailer trucks.

- **The cab and engine** of a trailer truck is called the tractor unit. The load is carried in the trailer.

- **In Australia** one tractor may pull several trailers in a "road-train" along the long, straight desert roads.

- **The longest truck** is the Arctic Snow Train, first made for the U.S. army. This is 570 ft (174 m) long and has 54 wheels.

- **Large trucks** are sometimes called "juggernauts." Juggernaut was a form of the Hindu god Vishnu who rode a huge chariot, supposed by Europeans to crush people beneath its wheels.

29

Buses and coaches

▲ *Like most early buses, this one from the early 1920s was built by adding a coach body to a truck base.*

- **Horse-drawn stagecoaches** were the first regular public coach services between two or more points or "stages." They were first used in London during the 1630s.

- **Stagecoaches** reached their heyday in the early 1800s when new tarred roads made travel faster. Coaches went from London to Edinburgh in 40 hours.

- **Bus is short** for "omnibus" which means "for all" in latin. The word first came into use in Paris in the 1820s for big coaches carrying lots of people on shorter, local trips.

- **In 1830** Goldsworthy Gurney put a steam engine in a coach to make the first powered bus. It operated four times a day between Cheltenham and Gloucester in England.

- **In the 1850s** British government laws restricted steam road vehicles, so big new cities developed horse buses.

- **In 1895** a gasoline-engine bus was built in Germany.

- **In 1904** the London General Omnibus Co. ran the first gasoline-engine bus services. The buses were double-decked.

- **In 1905** the first motor buses ran on New York's 5th Avenue.

- **In 1928** the first transcontinental bus service crossed the U.S.A.

- **From the 1950s** trailer buses were used in European cities. A trailer joined to the bus carries extra passengers.

◀ *Stagecoaches carried passengers, luggage, and mail over long distances.*

Streetcars and cable cars

- **Streetcars** are buses that run on rails laid through city streets. They are called trams in Britain.

- **Early streetcars** in the 1830s were pulled by horses. By the 1870s, horse-drawn streetcars were used in many cities.

- **In 1834** Thomas Davenport, a blacksmith from Vermont, built a battery-powered electric streetcar.

- **In 1860** an American called George Train set up battery-powered electric streetcar systems in London.

▶ *The original Hallidie cable car system dating from 1873 still runs in San Francisco.*

▶ *Some cable cars are used as ski lifts. They run on cables suspended between towers.*

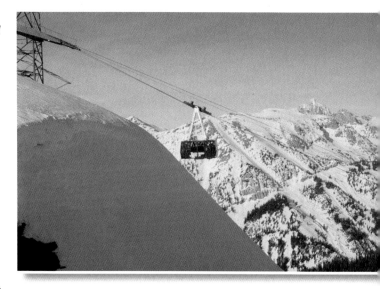

- **In 1873** Andrew Hallidie introduced cable cars in San Francisco. The cars were hauled by a cable running in a slot in the street. A powerhouse pulled the cable at a speed of 8.5 mph (14 km/h). Similar systems were built in many cities in the 1880s but were soon replaced by electric streetcars.

- **In 1888** Frank Sprague demonstrated a streetcar run from electric overhead cables in Richmond, Virginia.

- **In most U.S. streetcars,** electric current was picked up via a long pole with a small wheel called a shoe that slid along the cable. The pick-up was called a trolley. Many European streetcars, however, picked up current via a collapsible frame called a pantograph.

- **In the early 1900s,** electric streetcar systems were set up in most world cities.

- **In the 1930s** most cities, except in eastern Europe and Russia, replaced streetcars with buses.

- **In the 1990s** some cities, like Manchester in England, built new streetcar systems, because they are fume-free.

Moving on snow

- **Vehicles** designed to move on snow are supported on flat boards called runners, skids, or skis. These slide over snow easily and spread the vehicle's weight over a larger area.

- **Sleds or sleighs** drawn by horses or dogs may have been the first vehicles ever used by humans.

- **Cutters** are light, graceful horse-drawn sleighs first introduced in the U.S.A. about 1800.

- **Troikas** are Russian sleighs (or carriages) drawn by three horses. The middle horse is supposed to trot while the outer horses gallop in particular ways.

▲ *Cutters are still used in the north-eastern U.S.A. as a charming way of getting around in the winter snows.*

▶ *A skidoo is a motorized sled driven on snowy surfaces.*

- **Native Americans** had toboggans made of poles tied with leather thongs.

- **Snowmobiles** are vehicles with two skis at the front and a motor-driven track roll at the back. Racing snowmobiles can reach over 100 mph (160 km/h).

- **Snowmobiles** are steered by handlebars that control the skis and by the shifting of the driver's weight.

- **The first propeller-driven** snowmobile was built in the 1920s. Tracked snowmobiles were developed in 1959 by Canadian Joseph Bombardier.

- **In the 1960s** carved wooden skis dating back 8,000 years were found in a bog at Vis near the Urals in Russia.

- **The earliest skates** were mostly small bone skis tied to the feet.

Tractors

- **Tractors** are motor vehicles used mostly on farms for pulling or pushing machines such as plows.

- **Tractors** are also used in factories, by the army, for heavy jobs like logging and for clearing snow.

> ...·FASCINATING FACT...·
> There are now well over 16 million tractors around the world.

▲ *An early tractor dating back to 1917.*

▲ *Modern tractors can be adapted to operate all kinds of devices, including this haybaler, via the power take-off.*

● **Steam-powered tractors** called "traction engines" were introduced in 1834 by Walter Hancock.

● **Traction-engines** could pull up to 40 plows at once via long chains, but they were too cumbersome to be practical in hilly country.

● **Gasoline-powered tractors** were introduced in the 1890s but they were not powerful enough for most farm work.

● **The first all-purpose** farm tractors appeared in the 1920s and soon began to replace horses and oxen.

● **Plows and other equipment** are drawn along via the towbar on the back of the tractor.

● **The power take-off** or PTO allows the tractor's engine to power equipment such as potato diggers.

● **Twenty-five percent of all tractors** are in the U.S.A.

The first railroads

- **Railroads** were invented long before steam power.
- **The Diolkos** was a 3.7 mi- (6 km-) long railroad that carried boats across the Corinthisthmus in Greece in the 6th-century BC. Trucks pushed by slaves ran in grooves in a limestone track.

- **The Diolkos** ran for over 1,300 years until AD900.

- **Railroads** were revived in the 14th century with wooden tracks to guide horse and hand carts taking ore out of mines.

- **In the 1700s** English ironmakers began to make rails using iron. First they used wood covered in iron. Then later, the whole rail was made of iron. Iron wheels with "flanges" (lips) ran inside the track.

◀ *The successful design of Trevithick's engine in 1804 meant that railroads became the main form of transportation.*

- **In 1804** English engineer Richard Trevithick built the first successful steam railroad locomotive.

- **Trevithick's** engine pulled a train of five wagons with 9 tons of iron and 70 men along 9 mi (15 km) of track at the Pendarren ironworks in Wales.

- **On September 27, 1825,** George and Robert Stephenson opened the world's first steam passenger railway, the Stockton and Darlington in England.

- **The gauge (track width)** used for the Stockton and Darlington was 4.7 ft (1.44 m), the same length as axles on horse-wagons. This became the standard gauge in the U.S.A. and much of Europe.

- **The English-built** *Stourbridge Lion* was the first full-size steam locomotive to run in the U.S.A. It ran on wooden track in Pennsylvania in 1829.

▲ *The Stephensons' Rocket was the most famous early locomotive, winning the first locomotive speed trials at Rainhill in England in 1829.*

Building the railroads

▲ *The new railroads often meant demolishing huge strips through cities to lay track into stations.*

- **On September 15, 1830** the world's first real passenger railroad opened between Liverpool and Manchester.

- **At the opening** of the Liverpool and Manchester railroad government minister William Huskisson was killed by the locomotive.

- **In 1831** the *Best Friend* started a regular train service between Charleston and Hamburg, South Carolina.

- **By 1835** there were over 1,000 mi (1,600 km) of railroads in the U.S.A.

- **In Britain** railroad building became a mania in the 1840s.

- **Hundreds of Acts of Parliament** gave railroad companies the powers to carve their way through cities and the countryside.

- **By the late 1840s** Great Western Railway trains were able to average well over 60 mph (100 km/h) all the way from London to Exeter via Bristol, completing the 180 mi (300 km) journey in under four hours.

- **On May 10, 1869** railroads from either side of the United States met at Promontory, Utah, giving North America the first transcontinental railroad.

- **The British** built 24,000 mi (40,000 km) of railways in India in the 1880s.

- **Vast armies of men** worked on building the railroads—45,000 on the London and Southampton railroad alone.

▲ *The Canadian Pacific Railway completed Canada's first transcontinental line in 1885.*

Steam locomotives

▶ The biggest and strongest steam locomotives ever were nicknamed "Big Boy." They were designed to haul 3,000-ton freight trains over the Rocky Mountains.

- **Steam locomotives** get their power by burning coal in a firebox. This heats up water in a boiler, making steam. The steam drives a piston back and forth and the piston turns the wheels via connecting rods and cranks.

- **It takes about three hours** for the crew to get up enough steam to get a locomotive moving.

- **Coal and water** are often stored in a wagon called a tender, towed behind the locomotive.

- **A tender** holds 10 tons of coal and 8,000 gal (30,000 l) of water.

- **Locomotive classes** are described by their wheel layout.

- **A 4-6-2** has four small leading "bogie" wheels, six big driving wheels, and two small trailing wheels. The small bogie wheels carry much of the weight.

- **The greatest** Victorian locomotive designer was James Nasmyth.

- **In the American Civil War** (1861–65) the locomotive *The General* was recaptured by Confederates after an epic chase in another locomotive.

- **The Flying Scotsman** was a locomotive designed by Sir Nigel Gresley (1876–1941). It pulled trains 380 mi (630 km) from London to Edinburgh in under six hours.

> **. . . . FASCINATING FACT . . . .**
> The first locomotive to hit 100 mph
> (160 km/h) was the City of Truro in 1895.

▼ *An American locomotive of the 1890s.*

Diesel trains

- **The diesel engine** was invented by Rudolf Diesel in 1892 and experiments with diesel locomotives started soon after. The first great success was the *Flying Hamburger* which ran from Berlin to Hamburg in the 1930s at speeds of 78 mph (125 km/h). Diesel took over from steam in the 1950s and 1960s.

- **Diesel locomotives** are really electric locomotives that carry their own power plant. The wheels are driven by an electric motor which is supplied with electricity by the locomotive's diesel engine.

Diesel engine in which diesel fuel is squeezed inside cylinders until it bursts into flame. The expansion of the fuel as it burns provides the engine's power

Cooling fan

Driver's cab

Direct Current electricity generator turned by the power of the diesel engine

Locomotive driving wheels, turned by the power of the electricity generator

Fuel tank carrying diesel fuel. Because a diesel train carries its fuel on board, it is entirely independent, unlike electric locomotives

▲ *This is a typical British diesel-electric locomotive from the 1960s. It has a cab at both ends so that it can be operated in either direction. This is one of the older generation of diesel-electrics that use DC (Direct Current) generators. DC generators give a current that flows in only one direction. Most newer engines take advantage of rectifiers to use the current from an AC (Alternating Current) generator. An AC generator gives a current that swaps direction many times a second. The rectifiers convert this into a direct current. AC generators are far more powerful and efficient.*

- **The power output of a diesel** engine is limited, so high-speed trains are electric. However, diesels can supply their own electricity so need no trackside cables.

- **There are two other kinds** of diesel apart from diesel-electrics: diesel-hydraulic and diesel-mechanical.

- **In diesel-hydraulics,** the power from the diesel engine is connected to the wheels via a torque converter, which is a turbine driven around by fluid.

- **In diesel-mechanicals,** the power is transmitted from the diesel engine to the wheels via gears and shafts. This only works for small locomotives.

- **Diesel locomotives** are made up of one or more separate units. An A unit holds the driver's cab and leads the train. A B unit simply holds an engine.

- **A typical diesel locomotive** for fast, heavy trains may consist of one A unit and six B units.

- **The usual maximum** power output from a single diesel locomotive is about 3,500–4,000 horsepower.

Electric trains

▲ *Electric current flows from the power line through conductors to the locomotive's motor.*

● **The first practical electric** trains date from 1879, but they only became widespread in the 1920s.

● **Electric locomotives** pick up electric current either from a third "live" rail or from overhead cables.

● **To pick up** power from overhead cables, locomotives need a spring-loaded frame or pantograph to keep in contact.

● **Electric trains** are clean and powerful and are also able to travel faster than other trains.

● **Older systems** mostly used Direct Current (DC) motors, operating at 1,500–3,000 volts for overhead cables and 700 volts for live rails.

▶ *Japan's Shinkansen "bullet train" was the first of the modern high-speed electric trains, regularly operating at speeds of over 250 mph (400 km/h).*

- **High-speed trains** like France's TGV and Japan's Shinkansen use "three-phase" Alternating Current (AC) motors operating at 25,000 volts.

- **The Paris–London** Eurostar works on 25,000 volt AC overhead cables in France, and 750 volt live rails after it comes out of the Channel Tunnel in England.

- **Magnetic levitation** or maglev trains do not have wheels but glide along supported by electromagnets.

- **In electrodynamic maglevs,** the train rides on repulsing magnets. In electromagnetic maglevs, they hang from attracting magnets.

- **Maglevs** are used now only for short, low-speed trains, but they may one day be the fastest of all. High-speed maglev developments now use "superconducting" electromagnets which are costly to make. But a new idea is to use long strings of ordinary permanent magnets.

Stations

▲ *Built in 1927, Union Station in Toronto was the largest station in Canada at the time.*

- **London Bridge** station is the oldest big city terminal, first built from wood in 1836, then of brick in the 1840s.

- **In the 19th century** railroad companies competed to make the grandest, most palatial railroad stations.

- **The Gare d'Orsay** in Paris was an incredibly luxurious station built in 1900 in what is called the Beaux Arts (beautiful arts) style. It is now a museum and gallery.

- **When first built** in 1890, Sirkeci in Istanbul—the terminal of the Orient Express—glittered like an oriental palace.

- **Bombay's Victoria**—now Chhatrapati Sivaji—is a palatial gothic station, built in 1888 over a shrine to Mumba Devi, who was the goddess of the original inhabitants of Bombay.

- **Grand Central Station** in New York cost a staggering $43 million to build in 1914.

- **Liverpool Street Station** in London was built in 1874 on the site of the 13th century Bedlam hospital for lunatics.

- **London's St. Pancras** is a stunning Gothic building designed by George Gilbert Scott. It was built 1863–72.

- **Chicago's North Western** is a monument to the Jazz Age in the city, dating from 1911.

- **In April 1917**, Lenin returned to Russia and announced the start of the Russian Revolution at St. Petersburg's famous Finland railroad station.

▲ *The great hall at Grand Central Station in New York is one of the most spectacular railroad stations in the world.*

Underground railroads

- **Underground railroads** are also called subways, metros, or even just tubes.

- **There are three kinds:** open-cut; cut and cover, and tube.

- **Open-cut subways** are built by digging rectangular ditches in streets, like much of New York's subway.

- **Cut-and-cover subways** are when an open-cut subway is covered again with a road or pavement.

- **Tubes** are deep, round tunnels created by boring through the ground, like most of London's lines.

▲ *Underground railroads carry people quickly and avoid the heavy traffic found in city centers.*

▲ *London was the first city in the world to have an underground system. Much of it is now in deep tube tunnels.*

- **The world's first underground** was the cut-and-cover Metropolitan Line in London, opened on January 10, 1863, using steam engines.

- **In 1890** the world's first electric tube trains ran on London's first deep tube, the City and South London.

- **After 1900** American Charles Yerkes, builder of the Chicago Loop railway, helped give London the world's most extensive tube network with 140 mi (225 km) of deep tubes.

- **Moscow's Metro** grand stations were built in the 1930s with marble, stained glass, statues, and chandeliers.

- **New York City** has the world's largest subway network, but unlike London's most of it is quite shallow. The first line opened on October 27, 1904.

Famous trains

- **Pullman coaches** became a byword for luxury in the U.S.A. in the 1860s.

- **After a trip to the U.S.A.,** young Belgian George Nagelmackers set up the Wagon-Lits company to do in Europe as Pullman had in the U.S.A.

- **The most famous** Wagon-Lits train was the luxurious Orient-Express from Paris to Istanbul, which started in 1883.

- **Among the many famous** travelers on the Orient Express were the female spy Mata Hari, the fictional British spy James Bond, and 1940s film star Marlene Dietrich.

- **Another famous** Wagon-Lits train is the *Trans-Siberian Express*, which began in 1898.

- **The *Trans-Siberian*** takes eight days to go right across Russia and Siberia from Moscow to Vladivostok.

- **The *Flying Scotsman*** was famed for its fast, non-stop runs from London to Edinburgh in the 1920s.

- **The *Golden Arrow*** ran from London to Paris.

- **The *Indian Pacific*** in Australia runs on the world's longest straight track, 297 mi (478 km) across the Nullarbor Plain.

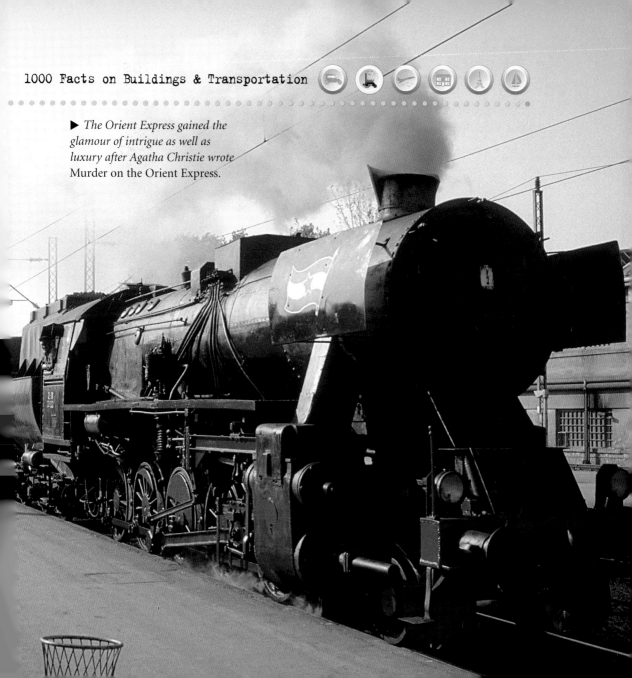

▶ *The Orient Express gained the glamour of intrigue as well as luxury after Agatha Christie wrote* Murder on the Orient Express.

Record-breaking trains

▶ *TGV Atlantiques often hit 186 mph (300 km/h) on the French part of the Eurostar run from Paris to London.*

- **The fastest steam train** ever was the *Mallard* designed by Gresley (see steam locomotives.) It pulled seven coaches at a speed of 125 mph (201 km/h) on July 3, 1938.

- **The most powerful** steam locomotive was the U.S. Virginian Railway No. 700. It pulled with a force of over 198,416lb (90,000kg).

- **The heaviest trains** ever pulled by a single locomotive were 250-truck trains that ran on the Erie Railroad in the U.S.A. from 1914 to 1929. They weighed over 15,000 tons.

- **The longest train** was a 4.5 mi (7.3 km) 660-truck train that ran from Saldanha to Sishen in South Africa on August 26, 1989.

- **The longest passenger train** was a 5,682 ft (1,732 m) 70-car train from Ghent to Ostend in Belgium on April 27, 1991.

- **The fastest diesel train** at 154 mph (248 km/h) was a British Rail Intercity 125 between Darlington and York on November 1, 1987.

- **The fastest scheduled service** is the Hiroshima to Kokura bullet train in Japan which covers 120 mi (192 km) in 44 minutes at an average 162.1 mi (261.8 km/h).

▲ *Bullet trains in a Tokyo train station.*

- **The TGV** from Lille to Roissy in France covers 126 mi (203 km) in 48 mins at an average 158 mph (254.3 km/h).

- **The fastest train speed ever** was 320.2 mph (515.3 km/h) by the TGV between Courtalain and Tours, France on May 18, 1990.

- **The fastest speed on rail** was 6,121 mph (9,851 km/h) by a rocket sled on White Sands Missile Range, New Mexico in October 1982.

Trains of the future

▲ *Maglev trains are suspended by powerful magnets above a guide track. It is thought Maglevs of the future may exceed 500 mph (800 km/h)!*

- **Monorails** are single-beam tracks raised over city streets.

- **The first monorail** was built in Wuppertal in Germany as long ago as 1901 and monorails have been seen as trains of the future ever since.

- **Monorails** of the future may be air-cushion trains or maglevs, as at Birmingham airport in England.

- **A maglev** is proposed in Japan to take passengers the 320 mi (515 km) from Tokyo to Osaka in under an hour. Germany's version is called Transrapid.

- **PRT** or Personalized Rapid Transport is a system of small vehicles that run on elevated tracks at high speed and are operated electrically.

- **185 mph (300 km/h) plus** High Speed Train (HST) systems like the French TGV are being built in many places. A line from Moscow to St. Petersburg was opened in 2000.

- **In 2004** the 200 mph (320 km/h) Tampa-Miami Florida Overland Express opens. The same year a 3,000 mi (4,500 km) 185 mph (300 km/h) line may also open from Melbourne to Darwin, Australia.

- **Most HSTs** run on special straight tracks. Tilting trains lean into bends to give high speeds on winding old tracks.

- **Tilting trains** include the 185 mph (300 km/h) Italian Fiat Pendolini and the Swedish-built X2000.

- **Since 2000**, the 150 mph (240 km/h) tilting train *The American Flyer*—Washington to Baltimore—has been the U.S.A.'s fastest train.

▶ *Many cities now have short monorails, but they seem unlikely to get much bigger because of the disruption the building work would cause.*

57

Airships

▼ *This is a cutaway of one of the new breed of small airships made from lightweight materials and filled with safe, non-flammable helium gas.*

Airbags or "ballonets" inside the helium-filled envelope. As the airship climbs, air pressure drops and the helium expands, pushing air out of the ballonets. As the airship drops again, the helium contracts and air is let into the ballonets again

Rigid envelope shell

Envelope filled with helium

Elevator flaps to help climbing or diving

Valve to let air in and out of the ballonets

Gondola where pilot sits

Landing wheel

Propeller powered by a car engine

Rudder to steer the airship to the left or right

- **By the mid-1800s** ballooning was a popular activity. In 1852, French engineer Henri Giffard made a cigar-shaped balloon filled with the very light gas hydrogen. He powered it with a steam-driven propeller and added a rudder to make it more "dirigible" or steerable.

> **FASCINATING FACT**
> Fighter planes could take off from and land on the 1930s airship Akron in mid-air.

- **In 1884** two French inventors, Charles Renard and Arthur Krebs, built the first dirigible balloon, *La France*. This was powered by an electric motor.

- **In 1897** Austrian David Schwartz gave a powered, cigar-shaped balloon a rigid frame to create the first airship.

- **In 1900** Count Ferdinand von Zeppelin built the first of his huge airships, the 420 ft- (128 m-) long LZ-1.

- **In 1909** Zeppelin helped set up the first airline, DELAG, flying 485 ft- (148 m-) long airships, carrying 10,000 passengers in its first four years.

- **In World War I**, Germany used Zeppelin airships to scout enemy positions and make the first aerial bombing raids.

- **By the 1920s** vast airships were carrying people back and forth across the Atlantic in the style of a luxury oceanliner. The *Graf Zeppelin* flew at 80 mph (130 km/h.) In its gondola, 60 or more passengers sat in comfortable lounges, walked to cocktail bars, or listened to bands playing.

- **On May 6, 1937** disaster struck the giant 800 ft- (245 m-) long airship *Hindenburg* as it docked at Lakehurst, New Jersey. The hydrogen in its balloon caught fire and exploded, killing 35 people. The day of the airship was over.

- **In recent years** there has been a revival of airships for advertising, filled with safer helium gas.

Biplanes

▲ *Felix du Temple built a person-carrying steam-powered monoplane in 1874.*

- **Most early planes** were biplanes (double-wingers) or even triplanes (triple-wingers).

- **Monoplanes** (single-wingers) like Blériot's (see record-breaking flights) were fast and won many early races—because they did not drag on the air like multi-wings.

- **Accidents** by overstressed competition monoplanes made it look as if they were dangerous. Single wings were weak, it seemed, because they had to be very long to give a similar lifting area to multi-wings.

- **In 1912** the French and British banned monoplanes, so all World War I fighter planes were multi-wingers.

▶ *The biplanes of World War I were slow but highly maneuverable. Pilots were able to show tremendous flying skill in the first aerial "dog fights" between planes.*

- **Biplane wings** were strong because struts and wires linked the small, light wings to combine their strength.

- **Famous World War I** fighters included the British Sopwith Camel and Bristol Fighter.

- **The Fokker triplane** flown by German air ace Baron von Richtofen (the Red Baron) was said to be "fearsome to look at and climbs like an elevator."

- **With their network** of struts and wires, biplanes were affectionately known as "string bags."

- **In the years** after World War I, huge biplane airliners were built including the Handley Page Heracles.

- **By the late 1920s** planes could be built strongly all in metal. So to cut drag and boost speed designers went back to monoplanes with planes like the Supermarine S6B. Soon biplanes seemed old-fashioned.

The Wright brothers

▲ *One of the five who witnessed the flight took this picture. But apart from a report in "Popular Science" the Wrights' success was little known about for five years.*

- **The Wright brothers**, Orville and Wilbur, built the world's first successful plane, the *Flyer*.

- **On December 17, 1903** the Wright brothers made the first powered, long and controlled airplane flight at Kitty Hawk, North Carolina.

- **Wilbur Wright** was born in 1867 on a farm near New Castle, Indiana; Orville was born in 1871 in Dayton, Ohio.

- **The Wright brothers** began as bicycle-makers but became keen on flying after hearing about the death of pioneer glider Otto Lilienthal in 1896.

- **From 1899 to 1903** they worked at Kitty Hawk methodically improving their design and flying skill.

- **Many early planes** took off but lacked control. The key to the Wrights' success was stopping the plane from rolling, using wires to "warp" (twist) the wings to lift one side or the other.

- **The *Flyer*'s** wing warp meant it could not only fly level but make balanced, banked turns (like a bicycle cornering).

- **For the first flight** Orville was at the controls.

- **The historic first flight** lasted 12 seconds, in which the *Flyer* traveled 120 ft (37 m) and landed safely.

- **On October 5, 1905** the Wrights flew 24 mi (38.9 km) in 38 minutes.

▶ *Orville and Wilbur Wright's first airplane cost less than $1,000 to build.*

Bombers of World War II

◄ The Stuka was the most famous dive-bomber used by the Germans in World War II.

- **In the 1930s** Boeing built the B-17 *Flying Fortress*, bristling with gun turrets to battle its way through to targets even by day.

- **The 1929** Curtis F8C Helldiver was the first "dive-bomber"—designed to drop its bombs at the end of a long dive on targets like aircraft carriers. German "Stuka" dive-bombers gained a fearsome name in the German invasions of 1939.

- **The twin-engined** Heinkel III, Dornier Do17, and Junkers Ju88 were the main German bombers in the Blitzkrieg (literally "lightning war") raids of the Battle of Britain.

- **In December 1939** the heavy loss of British Wellingtons showed that lightly armed bombers could not sustain daylight raids, so the British switched to night raids.

- **Blind-bombing** radar systems like the Hs2, and flare trails left by advance "Pathfinder" missions, improved accuracy on night raids.

- **The ultra-light** De Havilland Mosquito was fast enough to fly daylight raids.

- **The Russian Ilyushin Il-2** or Stormovik was so good at bombing tanks Stalin said it was "as necessary to the Red Army as air or bread."

- **The dambusters** were the Lancasters of 617 squadron of 1943 that attacked German dams with "bouncing bombs." These were round bombs designed by Barnes Wallis that bounced over the water surface toward the target dams.

- **Kamikaze** (Japanese for "divine wind") were fighters loaded with bombs and gasoline which their pilots aimed in suicide dives at enemy ships.

▲ *The British Avro Lancaster could carry 6.6 tons of bombs on low altitude raids.*

- **The biggest bomber** was the Boeing B-29 *Superfortress* which could fly over 32,000 ft (10,000 m) up. In 1945, B-29s dropped atomic bombs on Hiroshima and Nagasaki in Japan.

Fighters of World War II

- **World War II** fighter planes were sleek monoplanes (single-winged aircraft) very different from the biplanes of World War II. Many were developed from racing machines of the 1920s and 1930s.

- **The most famous** British plane was the Supermarine Spitfire. This was developed from the S.6B seaplane which won the coveted Schneider trophy in the late 1920s.

- **The most famous American** fighter was the North American P-51 Mustang, which could reach speeds of over 435 mph (700 km/h) and had a range of 1,000 mi (1,700 km). It was widely used as an escort for bombers.

- **In the Pacific** U.S. planes like the Grumman Wildcat and Hellcat fought against the fast and highly maneuverable Japanese Mitsubishi A6M "Zero."

- **The most famous German** fighter was the fast, agile Messerschmitt Bf 109. This was the plane flown by German air ace Erich Hartmann, who shot down 352 enemy planes. Over 33,000 were made during the war.

- **Me 109s** were nicknamed by model. The Bf109E was the Emil. The Bf109G was the Gustav.

- **The German Focke-Wulf** had a big BMW radial engine that enabled it to climb over 0.7 mi (1.1 km) a minute.

- **The most famous Soviet** fighter was the MiG LaGG-3 Interceptor, flown by Soviet air ace Ivan Kozhedub who shot down 62 German planes.

- **The British Hawker Hurricane** was more old-fashioned, slower, and less famous than the Spitfire, but its reliability made it highly effective. Hurricanes actually destroyed more enemy aircraft than Spitfires.

Radio antenna

All metal wings with a
wingspan of 33 ft (10 m)

Bulletproof windshield

Self-sealing fuel tanks

Four machine guns
in each wing

One 20 mm cannon
in each wing

1,030 hp Rolls-Royce Merlin
engine capable of powering the
plane to over 325 mph (520 km/h)

Three-blade
propeller

▲ Along with the Spitfire, the
Hurricane was the mainstay of the
British defense against the German air
invasion in the Battle of Britain in
1940. Hurricanes and Spitfires would
have spectacular aerial "dogfights" with
the Me 109s escorting the German
bombers. The sturdy Hurricane proved
a highly effective fighter plane.

◄ In the dogfights of
the Battle of Britain, the
Spitfire's 400 mph (650 km/h)
top speed and amazing agility
proved decisive.

Warplanes

- **The 540 mph (870 km/h)** German Messerschmitt Me 262 was the first jet fighter. It had straight wings like propeller planes.

- **The Lockheed Shooting Star** was the first successful U.S. jet fighter.

- **The Korean War** of the 1950s saw the first major combat between jet fighters. Most now had swept-back wings, like the Russian MiG-15 and the U.S. F-86 Saber.

- **In 1954** Boeing introduced the B-52 Superfortress, still the USAF's main bomber because of its huge bomb-carrying capacity.

- **In the 1950s** aircraft began flying close to the ground to avoid detection by radar. On modern ground-hugging planes like the Lockheed F-111 a computer radar system flies the plane automatically at a steady height over hills and valleys. If the system fails, the plane climbs automatically.

▲ *Pilots fly modern jets at supersonic speeds aided by laser-guided weapons, night-vision goggles, and other high-tech equipment.*

▲ *The world's fastest warplane is the Russian MiG-25, which has been tracked by radar flying at over 1,865 mph (3,000 km/h).*

- **The Hawker Harrier** of 1968 was the only successful "jump jet" with swiveling jets for vertical take-off (VTOL).

- **Airborne Early Warning** systems (AEWs) look down from above and detect low-flying aircraft. To evade them the U.S. began developing "stealth" systems like RCS and RAM.

- **RCS** or Radar Cross Section means altering the plane's shape to make it less obvious to radar. RAM (Radar Absorbent Material) is a coating that doesn't reflect radar.

- **In 1988** the U.S. unveiled its first "stealth" bomber, the B-2, codenamed Have Blue. The F117 stealth fighter followed.

- **The 1,550 mph (2,500 km/h) Russian Sukhoi S-37** Berkut ("golden eagle") of 1997 uses Forward Swept Wings (FSW) for maximum agility, rather than stealth technology.

69

Taking off

▶ *An F-15 preparing for take-off.*

- **An aircraft's wings** or "foils" are lifted by the air flowing above and beneath them as they slice through the air.

- **Because the top** of the wing is curved, air pushed over the wing speeds up and stretches out. The stretching of the air reduces its pressure.

- **Underneath the wing** air slows down and bunches up, the air pressure in this area rises.

- **The wing gains "lift"** as the air around the wing is sucked from above and pushed from below.

- **The amount of lift** depends on the angle of the wing—called the angle of attack—and its shape, and also how fast it is moving through the air.

- **Aircraft** get extra lift for climbing by increasing their speed through the air and by dropping the tail so that the main wings cut through the air at a steeper angle.

- **If the angle of attack** becomes too steep, the airflow breaks up and the wing loses lift. This is called a stall.

- **Planes** take off when air is moving fast enough over the wing to provide enough lift.

- **Airliners** have "high-lift" slots and flaps on the wings to give extra lift for slow takeoff and landing speeds.

. . . FASCINATING FACT . . .
Slots on the wing's leading edge smooth airflow to increase the safe angle of attack.

▲ *The high-lift flaps are down to give extra lift on a climb.*

71

Controlling
a plane

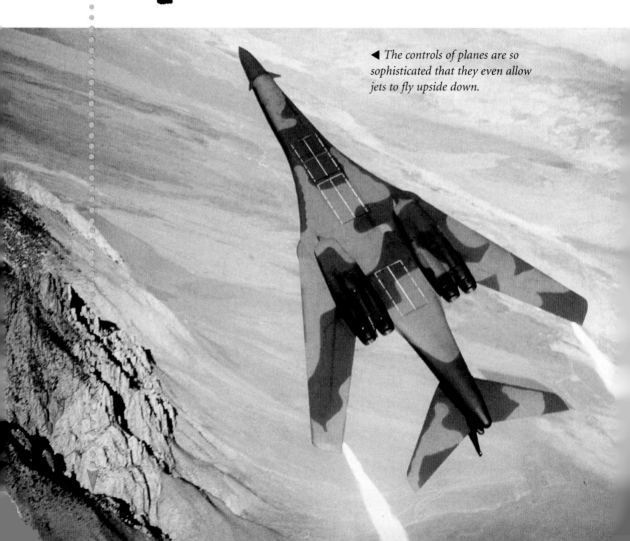

◀ *The controls of planes are so sophisticated that they even allow jets to fly upside down.*

- **A plane** is controlled in the air by moving hinged flaps on its wings and tail.

- **Changing pitch** is when the plane goes nose-up or nose-down to dive or climb.

- **Rolling** is when the plane rolls to one side, dipping one wing or the other.

- **Yawing** refers to when the plane steers to the left or right like a car.

- **Pitch** is controlled by raising or lowering hinged flaps on the rear wings called elevators.

▲ *In old-fashioned planes, the pilot controlled the flaps manually by moving a control stick linked to cables. In modern planes, the flaps are controlled automatically via electric wires (fly-by-wire) or laser beams (fly-by-light). The flight deck of this plane from 30 years ago has lots of dials to help the pilot. Modern planes have "glass cockpits," which means they have computer screens.*

- **To pitch up** in a small or simple plane, the pilot pulls back on the control column to raise the elevators.

- **Rolling** is controlled by large hinged flaps on the wings called ailerons.

- **To roll left** the pilot pushes the control column to the left, which raises the aileron on the left wing and lowers it on the right.

- **Yawing** is controlled by the vertical hinged flap on the tail called the rudder.

- **To yaw left** the pilot pushes the foot-operated rudder bar forward with his left foot, to swing the rudder left.

Jet engines

- **A kind of jet engine** was built by the Ancient Greek Hero of Alexander in the first century AD. It was a ball driven around by jets of steam escaping from two nozzles.

- **The first jet engines** were built at the same time in the 1930s by Pabst von Ohain in Germany and Frank Whittle in Britain—though neither knew of the other's work.

- **Ohain's engine** was put in the Heinkel HE-178 which first flew on August 27, 1939; Whittle's was put in the Gloster E28 of 1941. The first American jet was the Bell XP-59 Aircomet of 1942.

- **Jets** work by pushing a jet of air out the back. This hits the air so fast that the reaction thrusts the plane forward like a deflating balloon.

- **Jet engines** are also called gas turbines because they burn fuel gas to spin the blades of a turbine non-stop.

- **Turbojets** are the original form of jet engine. Air is scooped in at the front and squeezed by spinning "compressor" blades. Fuel sprayed into the squeezed air in the middle of the engine burns, making the mixture expand dramatically. The expanding air not only pushes round turbines which drive the compressor, but also sends out a high-speed jet of hot air to propel the plane. This high-speed jet is noisy but good for ultra-fast warplanes and the supersonic Concorde.

▲ *Like nearly all warplanes today, "stealth" aircraft are jet-propelled. But the afterburner stream of hot gases from the jets provides a "signature" that can show up all too clearly on some detection equipment. So stealth aircraft are designed to "supercruise"—that is, fly at supersonic speeds without much afterburn.*

The engine casing is made of carbon-fiber and plastic honeycomb for lightness. Inside is an outer bypass duct for the "cold stream" of air from the front fan. An inner duct takes the "hot stream" through the compressor, combustion chamber, and turbine to create the exhaust

Front fan to create "cold" bypass stream

▲ *All but the very fastest warplanes are powered by turbofan jet engines, like this Russian MiG jump jet. Turbofans first came into widespread use in the 1970s and are now by far the most common kind of jet engine.*

Exhaust where a hot jet of air roars out

- **Turboprops** are turbojets that use most of their power to turn a propeller rather than force out a hot air jet.

- **Turbofans** are used by most airliners because they are quieter and cheaper to run. In these, extra turbines turn a huge fan at the front. Air driven by this fan bypasses the engine core and gives a huge extra boost at low speeds.

- **Ramjets or** "flying stovepipes" are the simplest type of jet engine, used only on missiles. They dispense with both compressor and turbine blades and simply rely on the speed of the jet through the air to ram air in through the intake into the engine.

Airliners

▲ *The undercarriage consists of wheels upon which the airplane moves on the ground. Most high-speed planes retract (bring up) the wheels into the wings or fuselage after take-off.*

- **The Boeing 247** of 1933 was the world's first modern airliner, with smooth monoplane wings, streamlined metal body, and retractable landing wheels.

- **The Douglas DC-3** of 1936 could carry 21 passengers smoothly at 200 mph (320 km/h) and was the first popular airliner.

- **In 1952** the world's first jet airliner, the De Havilland Comet, came into service.

- **The Comet** more than halved international flight times but several tragic accidents led to its grounding in 1954. It flew again in 1958.

- **The age of jet** air travel really began with the American Boeing 707 and Douglas DC-8 of the late 1950s.

- **The Boeing 747** jumbo jet of 1970—the first "wide-bodied jet"—had over 400 seats, making air travel cheaper.

- **Four-engined jets** like the 747 can fly 6,000 mi (10,000 km) non-stop at speeds of 620 mph (1,000 km/h). Two- and three-engined jets, like the DC-10, make shorter flights.

- **Supersonic airliners** able to travel at over 1,250 mph (2,000 km/h) like the Anglo–French Concorde and Russian Tupolev Tu-144 have proved too heavy on fuel and too noisy.

- **The planned 555-seat Airbus** A380 would be the first double-deck airliner.

...**FASCINATING FACT**...
Spaceplanes like Lockheed–Martin's *Venture Star* may make space trips routine flights.

▲ *The four-engined Boeing 747 flies at 32,000–43,000 ft (10,000–13,000 m)—well above most storms—and can fly non-stop from New York to Tokyo.*

77

Airports

- **The world's first airport** was built at Croydon near London in 1928. Many early airports, like Berlin's, were social centers and attracted thousands of intrigued visitors.

- **Before airports** flying boats would land on water. So airports like New York's La Guardia were set close to water to take flying boats.

- **Over 50 airports** around the world now handle over ten million passengers a year each. Twenty-five of these are in the U.S.A.

- **Six airports** each handle over 30 million passengers, including Chicago's O'Hare and Hong Kong's Chep Lap Kok.

- **The world's largest** airport is King Abdul Aziz in Saudi Arabia. It covers 55,500 acres (22,464 hectares.) The U.S.A.'s biggest is Dallas. Europe's biggest is Paris's Charles de Gaulle.

- **Hong Kong's** Chep Lap Kok airport, opened in 1998, is one of the world's most modern.

- **Kansai** airport in Japan is built entirely on an artificial island in Osaka Bay so that it can operate 24 hours a day, without disturbing people with noise.

- **In early airports** terminals for each flight were set in a line, as at Kansas and Munich. But as flights increased, this layout meant passengers had a long way to walk.

- **Terminals in the 1970s** were set in extending piers like Amsterdam's Schiphol, or satellites like Los Angeles.

- **New airport terminals** like London's Stansted are set apart and linked by electric cars called "people-movers."

▶ *In the 1970s, Boeing 747 jumbo jets needed runways 2.5 mi (4 km) long to take-off, but better performance means they now need less.*

78

Rockets

- **Rockets** work by burning fuel. As fuel burns and swells out behind, the swelling pushes the rocket forward.

- **Solid-fuel rockets** are the oldest of all engines, used by the Chinese a thousand years ago.

- **Solid-fuel engines** are basically rods of solid, rubbery fuel with a tube down the middle.

- **Solid-fuel rockets** are usually only used for model rockets and small booster rockets. But the Space Shuttle has two solid-fuel rocket boosters (SRBs) as well as three main liquid-fuel engines.

- **Most powerful launch rockets** use liquid fuel. The Shuttle uses hydrogen. Other fuels include kerosene.

▶ *The mighty Atlas Rocket was used to launch America's first astronauts into space.*

- **Liquid fuel** only burns with oxygen, so rockets must also carry an oxidizer (a substance that gives oxygen) such as liquid oxygen (LOX) or nitrogen tetroxide.

> **FASCINATING FACT**
> The Saturn V rocket that launched the Apollo mission to the Moon is the most powerful rocket ever built.

- **Future rocket drives** include nuclear thermal engines that would use a nuclear reactor to heat the gas blasted out.

- **NASA's Deep Space-1** project is based on xenon ion engines which thrust electrically charged particles called ions, not hot gases, out of the back of the craft.

- **Solar thermal engines** of the future would collect the Sun's rays with a large mirror to heat gases.

▶ *Only powerful rockets can give the thrust to overcome gravity and launch spacecraft into space. They fall away in three stages once the spacecraft is traveling fast enough.*

Missiles

▼ *Ninety percent of the weight of a ballistic missile is the rocket propellant needed to reach its distant target.*

● **In AD1232** the Chinese defended the city of K'ai-feng against the Mongols with gunpowder rockets.

● **In the early 1800s** British army officer William Congreve developed metal rockets carrying explosives.

● **In World War II** the Germans developed the first guided missiles—missiles steered to their target in flight.

● **The most frightening** German guided missiles were the V-1 flying bombs or "doodlebugs" and the V-2 supersonic rockets. The V-2s flew at 3,295 mph (5,300 km/h).

● **Ballistic missiles** arch through the air like a thrown ball. Rockets propel them on the upward trajectory (path). They then coast down on their target. Cruise missiles are propelled by jet on a low flat path all the way.

● **In the 1950s** the U.S.A. and Soviet Union competed to develop long-range ICBMs (Intercontinental Ballistic Missiles) armed with nuclear warheads.

....FASCINATING FACT....

American Tomahawk cruise missiles could be aimed through goalposts at both ends of a football field 300 mi (500 km) away.

- **In the 1960s** antiballistic missiles were developed to shoot down missiles.

- **Some ICBMs** have a range of over 3,000 mi (5,000 km). Short-range missiles (SRBMs) like Pershings reach up to 300 mi (500 km).

- **SAMs** (surface-to-air missiles) like Redeye are fired from the ground at aircraft. Some can be fired by a soldier with a backpack. AAMs (air-to-air missiles) like Sidewinders are fired from planes for use against other planes.

▶ *Rocket missiles can carry nuclear warheads or other weapons halfway around the world.*

83

Supersonic planes

- **Supersonic planes** travel faster than the speed of sound.

- **The speed of sound** is about 760 mph (1,220 km/h) at sea level at 59°F (15°C).

- **Sound travels** slower higher up, so the speed of sound is about 670 mph (1,060 km/h) at 40,000 ft (12,000 m).

- **Supersonic** plane speeds are given in Mach numbers. These are the speed of the plane divided by the speed of sound at the plane's altitude.

- **A plane flying** at 932 mph (1,500 km/h) at 40,000 ft (12,000 m), where the speed of sound is 670 mph (1,060 km/h), is at Mach 1.46.

- **A plane flying** at supersonic speeds builds up shock waves in front and behind because it keeps catching up and compressing the sound waves in front of it.

- **The double shock waves** create a sharp crack called a sonic boom that is heard on the ground. Two booms can often be heard one or two seconds apart.

▲ *In 1976 Concorde became the first supersonic aircraft to carry passengers on commercial flights.*

- **In 1947** Chuck Yeager of the USAF made the first supersonic flight in the Bell X-1 rocket plane. The X-15 rocket plane later reached speeds faster than Mach 6. Speeds faster than Mach 5 are called hypersonic.

- **The first jet plane** to fly supersonic was the F-100 Super Saber fighter of 1953. The first supersonic bomber was the USAF's Convair B-58 Hustler first used in 1956.

▼ *Supersonic jet fighter planes are used by the military to intercept and attack enemy aircraft.*

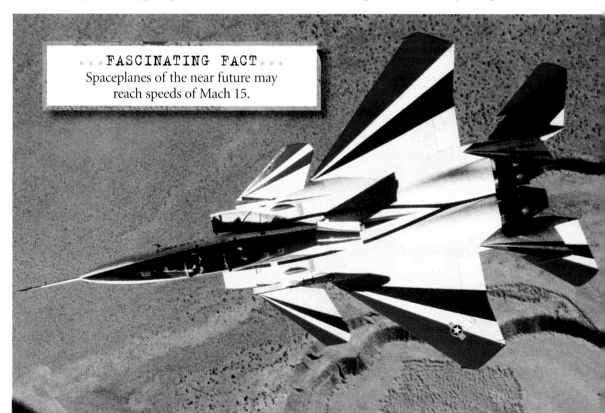

. . . FASCINATING FACT . . .
Spaceplanes of the near future may
reach speeds of Mach 15.

Record-breaking flights

- **On July 25, 1909** Louis Blériot made the first flight across the English Channel in a plane he built himself.

- **On May 8–31, 1919** (with stops) Capt A.C. Read and his crew made the first flight across the Atlantic in a Curtiss flying boat.

- **On June 14–15, 1919** John Alcock and Arthur Brown made the first non-stop flight across the Atlantic in an open cockpit Vickers Vimy biplane.

- **On November 12 to December 10, 1921** brothers Keith and Ross Smith made the first flight from England to Australia.

- **In February 1921** William Corey was the first person to fly solo across the United States.

- **In 1927** Frenchman Louis Breguet made the first flight across the South Atlantic.

▼ *Alcock and Brown's flight from Newfoundland to Ireland took 15 hours 57 minutes for the 1,950 mile journey.*

> **...FASCINATING FACT...**
> In December 1986, the American
> plane *Voyager*, piloted by Dick
> Rutan and Jeana Yeager, flew around
> the world non-stop in nine days.

▲ *Louis Bleriot's first flight across the English Channel in 1909.*

- **On May 21, 1927** American Charles Lindbergh made the first solo flight across the Atlantic in the *Spirit of St Louis*.

- **In July 1931** Wiley Post made the fastest round-the-world flight yet.

- **The story of Post's epic flight** was recorded in the book *Round the World in Eight Days*.

Helicopters

Without a tail rotor, the helicopter would spin around the opposite way to the main rotors. This is called torque reaction. The tail rotor also acts as a rudder to swing the tail left or right

To fly up or down, the pilot alters the angle or "pitch" of the main rotor blades with the "collective pitch" control. When the blades cut through the air almost flat, they give no lift and the helicopter sinks. To climb, the pilot steepens the pitch to increase lift

The angle of the blades is changed via rods linked to a sliding collar round the rotor shaft, called the swashplate

To fly forward or back, or for a banked turn, the pilot tilts the whole rotor with the "cyclic pitch" control

Rockets

Tail rotor drive shaft

Engine

Stabilizers

▲ A helicopter's rotor blades are really long, thin wings. The engine whirls them around so that they cut through the air and provide lift just like conventional wings (see taking off). But they are also like propellers, hauling the helicopter up just as a propeller pulls a plane.

- **Toy helicopters** have been around for centuries, and those made by air pioneer Sir George Cayley in the early 19th century are the most famous.

- **On November 13, 1907** a primitive helicopter with two sets of rotors lifted French mechanic Paul Cornu off the ground for 20 seconds.

- **The problem** with pioneer helicopters was control. The key was to vary the pitch of the rotor blades.

- **In 1937** German designer Heinrich Focke built an aircraft with two huge variable pitch rotors instead of wings and achieved a controlled hover. Months later, German Anton Flettner built the first true helicopter.

- **Focke and Flettner's** machines had two rotors turning in opposite directions to prevent torque reaction. In 1939, Russian-born American Igor Sikorsky solved the problem by adding a tail rotor.

- **The Jesus nut** that holds the main rotor to the shaft got its name because pilots said, "Oh Jesus, if that nut comes off..."

- **The biggest helicopter** was the Russian Mil Mi-12 Homer of 1968 which could lift 44 tons up to 7,400 ft (2,255 m).

- **The fastest helicopter** is the Westland Lynx, which flew at 250 mph (402 km/h) on August 6, 1986.

- **The Boeing/Sikorsky RAH-66** Comanche unveiled in 1999 is the first helicopter using stealth technology (see warplanes). It is made of carbon-fiber and other composite materials, and the rotor hub is hidden.

▶ *The Vietnam War saw the rise of heavily armed helicopter gunships designed to hit targets such as tanks.*

Balloons

- **Balloons** are bags filled with a light gas or hot air—both so light that the balloon floats in the air.

- **Balloons** designed to carry people into the air are of two types: hot-air balloons and gas balloons filled with hydrogen or helium.

- **Hot-air balloons** have a burner that continually fills the balloon with warm air to keep it afloat.

- **To carry two people** a hot-air balloon must have a bag of about 2,225 cubic yd (1,700 cubic m) in volume.

- **Balloons** are normally launched at dusk or dawn when the air is quite calm.

◀ *Hot-air ballooning has become a popular sport since Ed Yost, Tracy Barnes and other Americans began to make the bags from polyester in the 1960s.*

- **As the air in the bag cools** the balloon gradually sinks. To maintain height, the balloonist lights the burner to add warm air again.

- **To descend quickly** the balloonist pulls a cord to let air out through a vent in the top of the bag.

- **The first flight** in a hot-air balloon was made in Paris on October 15, 1783 by French scientist Jean de Rozier in a balloon made by the Montgolfier brothers.

- **The first hydrogen gas balloon flight** was made in Paris on December 1, 1783 by Jacques Charles and one of the two brothers Robert who built the balloon.

- **On March 20, 1999** Swiss Bertran Piccard and British Brian Jones completed the first round-the-world hot-air balloon flight.

▶ *The Montgolfier balloon was built from paper and silk.*

Autogiros
and microlights

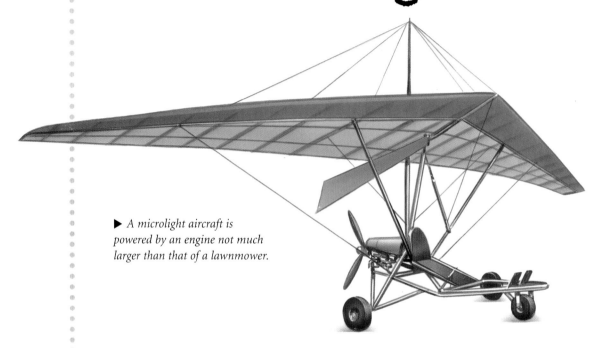

▶ *A microlight aircraft is powered by an engine not much larger than that of a lawnmower.*

- **In the 1400s** many European children played with flying toys kept aloft by whirling blades.

- **The autogiro** was built in 1923 by the Spanish inventor Juan de la Cierva.

- **An autogiro** is lifted, not by wings, but by turning rotor blades.

- **A helicopter uses** a powerful motor to turn the rotors; an autogiro's rotors are turned around by the pressure of air as the plane flies forward.

- **The autogiro** is pulled forward by propeller blades on the front like an ordinary small plane.

- **The autogiro** can fly at up to 140 mph (225 km/h), but cannot hover.

- **In the U.S.A. and Australia** microlights are called ultralights. They are small, very light aircraft.

- **The first microlight** was a hang-glider with a chainsaw motor, built by American hang-glider pioneer Bill Bennett in 1973.

- **Some microlights** have flexible fabric wings like hang-gliders.

- **Some microlights** have fixed wings with control flaps to steer them in flight.

▲ *For a while in the 1930s, many people believed autogiros would be the Model T Fords of the air—aircraft for everyone.*

93

Parachutes and hang-gliders

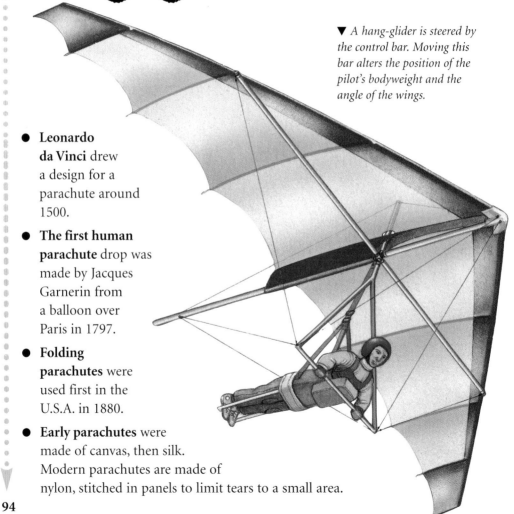

▼ *A hang-glider is steered by the control bar. Moving this bar alters the position of the pilot's bodyweight and the angle of the wings.*

- **Leonardo da Vinci** drew a design for a parachute around 1500.

- **The first human parachute** drop was made by Jacques Garnerin from a balloon over Paris in 1797.

- **Folding parachutes** were used first in the U.S.A. in 1880.

- **Early parachutes** were made of canvas, then silk. Modern parachutes are made of nylon, stitched in panels to limit tears to a small area.

94

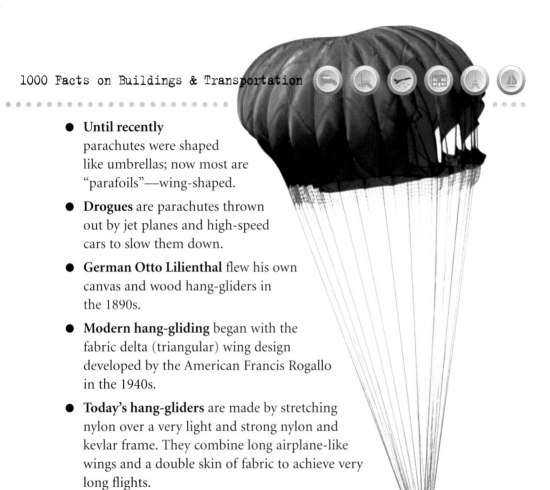

- **Until recently** parachutes were shaped like umbrellas; now most are "parafoils"—wing-shaped.

- **Drogues** are parachutes thrown out by jet planes and high-speed cars to slow them down.

- **German Otto Lilienthal** flew his own canvas and wood hang-gliders in the 1890s.

- **Modern hang-gliding** began with the fabric delta (triangular) wing design developed by the American Francis Rogallo in the 1940s.

- **Today's hang-gliders** are made by stretching nylon over a very light and strong nylon and kevlar frame. They combine long airplane-like wings and a double skin of fabric to achieve very long flights.

- **The first hang-gliders** achieved a glide ratio of 1:2.5. That is, they traveled only 2.5m forward for every 1m that they dropped. Today's hang-gliders give glide ratios of 1:14 or better.

▶ *Parachutes came into their own with the huge parachute drops of troops into battle during World War II. Parachutes are widely used in modern naval exercises as demonstrated by this U.S. Navy SEAL.*

Cathedrals

- **Cathedrals** are the churches of Christian bishops.

- **The word cathedral** comes from the Greek word for "seat," *kathedra.*

- **Cathedrals** are typically built in the shape of a cross. The entrance of the cathedral is at the west end.

- **The long end** of the cross is the nave. The short end, containing the altar and choir stalls, is called the apse. The arms of the cross are called transepts.

▶ *Paris's famous Notre Dame dates from 1163, but was remodeled in the 1840s by Viollet-le-Duc.*

- **A few cathedrals** were built as early as the 6th century AD. However, most of the cathedrals in Europe were built between 1000 and 1500.

- **Medieval cathedrals** were often built in the "gothic" style with soaring, pointed arches, tall spires, and huge pointed arch windows.

- **Many gothic cathedrals** have beautiful stained-glass windows. The famous Cathedral at Chartres in France has 176.

- **The modern Crystal Cathedral** in California is star-shaped and made of glass for TV broadcasts.

- **The world's tallest** cathedral spire is in Ulm, Germany, which is 528 ft (160.9 m) tall.

- **The world's smallest** cathedral is Christ Church in Highlandville, Missouri, which is just 13.7 by 17 ft (4.2 by 5.2 m) and holds only 18 people.

▼ *Ulm Cathedral was begun in 1377 but the immense stone tower at its western end was not completed until 1890.*

97

Castles

- **Castles** were the fortress homes of powerful men such as kings and dukes in the Middle Ages. The castle acted as a stronghold for commanding the country around it. They were also barracks, prisons, and armories.

- **The first castles** in the 11th century, had a high earth mound called a motte, topped by a wooden tower. Around this was an enclosure called a bailey, protected by a fence of wooden stakes and a ditch.

- **From the 12th century** the tower was built of stone and called a keep or donjon. This was the last refuge in an attack. Soon the wooden fences were replaced by thick stone walls and strong towers.

- **Walls and towers** were topped by battlements—low walls with gaps for defenders to fire weapons from.

- **Castles evolved** from a simple square tower to elaborate rings of fortifications. The entrance or gatehouse was equipped with booby traps.

- **From the 13th century** the ditch around the castle was often dug deep, filled with water, and called a moat.

- **Many castles** in England and Wales were first built by the Norman conquerors in the 11th century, including Windsor Castle.

- **In early castles** there was just a single great hall. Later castles had extra small rooms for the lord and lady, such as the solar, which had windows.

- **The gong farmer** was the man who had to clean out the pit at the bottom of the garderobe (toilet shute).

- **An attack** on a castle was called a siege and could last months, or even years.

▶ *This shows some of the main features of a medieval castle. Very few castles had all of these features. Innovations were constantly being added over the centuries as attackers came up with better ways of breaching the defenses and defenders found ways to hold them at bay.*

Drawbridge: a wooden bridge that was hauled up when the castle was attacked

The largest room was the great hall where people ate, slept, and carried on castle business

Staircases spiraled clockwise so that a defender could retreat, swinging his sword in his right hand

A few castles had private rooms on the third floor for the lord and his lady. Here the lady had her room or "bower"

Drop-gate or portcullis

Undercroft

Outer bailey

Gatehouse

Inner bailey

Chapel

Keep

Moat

Archers fire through a slit or loop

Famous castles

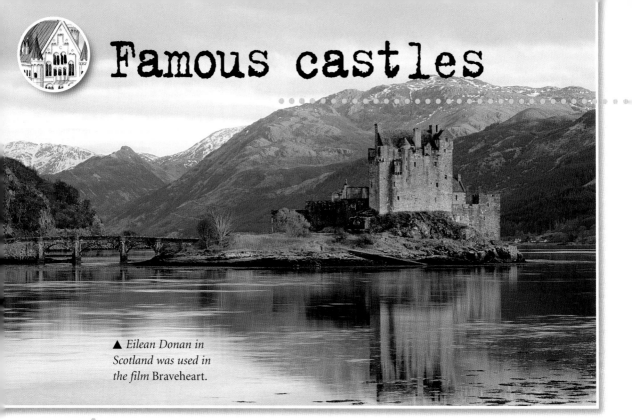

▲ *Eilean Donan in Scotland was used in the film* Braveheart.

- **The Arab Gormaz Castle** in the Castile region of Spain is Western Europe's biggest and oldest castle. It was started in 956AD by Caliph Al-Hakam II. It is 0.6 mi (1 km) round and over 1,300 ft (400 m) across.

- **Bran Castle** in Romania was built in 1212 by Teutonic (German) knights. In the 1450s, it was one of the castles used by Vlad the Impaler, the original Count Dracula.

- **Windsor Castle** in England has been one of the main homes of English kings and queens since the 1100s.

- **Malbork Castle** near Gdansk in Poland is the biggest medieval castle, built by the Teutonic knights in 1309.

- **Germany's Neuschwanstein Castle** was started in 1869 by "Mad" King Ludwig II. Its name means "new swan castle" after the Swan Knight in Wagner's opera *Lohengrin*.

- **Neuschwanstein** is the model for the castle in Walt Disney's cartoon film *Sleeping Beauty*.

- **15th century Blarney Castle** in Ireland is home to the famous "Blarney stone." Kissing the stone is said to give people the "gift of the gab" (fast and fluent talk).

- **Tintagel Castle** in Cornwall, England is where legend says the mythical King Arthur was conceived.

- **Colditz Castle** in Germany was a notorious prison camp in World War II.

  - **Carcassonne** in southern France is a whole town fortified by Catholics in about 1220 against those of the Cathar religion.

◀ *Ludwig II of Bavaria was eventually deposed by the government because of his overspending on elaborate buildings such as Neuschwanstein Castle.*

Skyscrapers

- **The first skyscrapers** were built in Chicago and New York in the 1880s.
- **A crucial step** in the development of skyscrapers was the invention of the first safety elevator by U.S. engineer Elisha Otis (1811–61) in 1857.
- **The Home Insurance Building** in Chicago, built in 1885, was one of the first skyscrapers.
- **In buildings** over 40 stories high, the weight of the building is less important in terms of strength than the wind load (the force of the wind against the building).
- **The Empire State Building** built in New York in 1931, was for decades the world's tallest building at 1,250 ft (381 m).

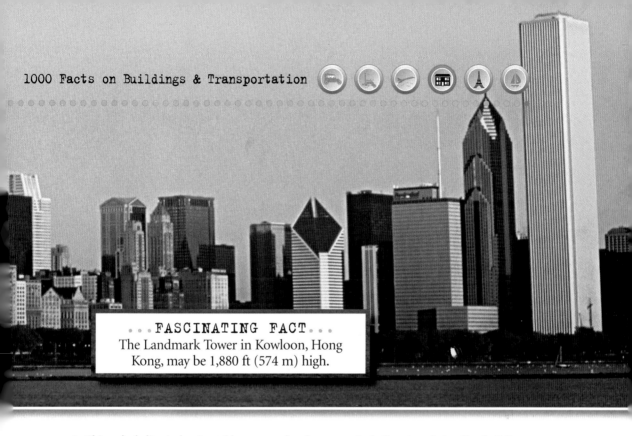

> ···FASCINATING FACT···
> The Landmark Tower in Kowloon, Hong
> Kong, may be 1,880 ft (574 m) high.

▲ *Chicago's skyline is dominated by spectacular skyscrapers including America's tallest building, the Sears Tower (left).*

- **In 2002, the tallest building** in America was the 1,450 ft- (442 m-) high Sears Tower in Chicago, built in 1974.

- **The world's tallest building** is the 1,780 ft (542 m) Petronas twin towers in Kuala Lumpur, Malaysia.

- **A tower** now being built in Sao Paolo in Brazil may be the world's tallest single tower at 1,625 ft (495 m).

- **If the Grollo Tower** is built in Australia, it will be 1,840 ft (560 m high).

103

Arches

- **Before arches** door openings were just two uprights spanned by a straight piece of wood or stone called a lintel.

- **Arches** replace a straight lintel with a curve. Curved arches can take more weight than a lintel, because downward weight makes a lintel snap in the middle.

- **The Romans** were the first to use round arches, so round arches are called Roman or Romanesque arches.

- **Roman arches** were built from wedge-shaped blocks of stone called voussoirs. They were built up from each side on a semi-circular wooden frame (later removed). A central wedge or keystone is slotted in at the top to hold them together.

- **The posts** supporting arches are called piers. The top of each post is called a springer.

▶ *The Gateway to the West is the world's tallest steel monument.*

104

▲ *The famous Arc de Triomphe in Paris was commissioned by Napoleon in 1806 in the style of the triumphal arches built in Ancient Rome to celebrate great victories.*

- **Pointed arches** were first used in Arab mosques like the Dome of the Rock in the 7th century.

- **Pointed arches** were brought to Europe from the Middle East by Crusader knights in the 1100s and put in churches to become part of the gothic style.

- **Horseshoe arches** are used in Islamic buildings all around the world.

- **The sides** of an ogee arch are S-shaped. Tudor arches are flattened ogees.

- **The world's biggest free-standing arch** is the Gateway to the West arch in St. Louis, Missouri. Completed in 1965, this arch is 630 ft (192 m) high and 630 ft (192 m) across.

Bridges

- **Rope suspension** bridges have been used for thousands of years. One of the first to use iron chains was the Lan Jin Bridge at Yunnan in China, built AD65.

- **The first all-iron bridge** was at Coalbrookdale, England. It was designed by Thomas Pritchard and built in 1779 by Abraham Darby.

- **In the early 1800s** Thomas Telford began building superb iron bridges such as Craigellachie over the Spey in Scotland (1814). He built Europe's first iron chain suspension bridge over the Menai Straits in Wales in 1826.

▲ *London's Tower Bridge was opened in 1894. It has a strong steel frame clothed in stone to support the two opening halves.*

- **Stephenson's Britannia railway bridge** of 1850, also over the Menai Straits, was the first hollow box girder bridge.

- **John Roebling's** Cincinnati suspension bridge was the world's longest bridge, at 1,056 ft (322 m) when built in 1866. Like all suspension bridges today, it was held up by iron wires, not chains. It was the prototype for his Brooklyn Bridge.

- **The Forth railway bridge** in Scotland was the world's first big cantilevered bridge.

- **In 1940** the Tacoma suspension bridge in Washington State was blown down by a moderate wind just months after its completion. The disaster forced engineers to make suspension bridges aerodynamic.

- **Aerodynamic design** played a major part in the design of Turkey's Bosphorus Bridge (1973) and England's Humber Bridge (1983).

- **In the 1970s** Japanese engineers began to build a kind of steel bridge which meant that by 2000 Japan had nine of the world's 20 longest bridges.

...FASCINATING FACT...

The Akashi–Kaikyo Bridge (1998), Japan, is the world's longest suspension bridge with a main span of 6,532 ft and two side spans of 3,150 ft.

▼ *Most bridges are now built of concrete and steel. These are some of the main kinds. The longest are normally suspension bridges, usually carrying roads, but Hong Kong's 4,518 ft- (1,377 m-) long Tsing Ma (1998) takes both road and rail.*

In cable-stayed bridges, the bridge hangs directly from steel cables

In suspension bridges the bridge hangs on steel wires on a cable suspended between tall towers. They are light so can be very long

Steel or concrete beam bridges are carried on piers. The beam may be a hollow steel girder through which cars and trains can run

In cantilevered bridges, each half of the bridge is balanced on a support

Bascule or lifting bridges like London's Tower Bridge swing up in the middle to allow tall ships through

Arch bridges are one of the oldest kinds and make very strong bridges

Bridges of wood and stone

- **The first bridges** were probably logs and vines slung across rivers to help people cross over.

- **The oldest known bridge** was an arch bridge built in Babylon about 2200BC.

- **Clapper bridges** are ancient bridges in which large stone slabs rest on piers (supports) of stone.

- **There are clapper bridges** in both Devon in England and Fujian in China.

- **The first brick bridges** were built by the Romans, like the Alcántara bridge over the Tagus River in Spain which was built around 100AD.

- **Long bridges** could be made with a series of arches linked together. Each arch is called a span.

- **Roman arches** were semi-circular, so each span was short; Chinese arches were flatter so they could span greater distances.

▲ *The Bridge of Sighs in Venice was built in 1600 to connect the Doge's prisons.*

▲ *The Ponte Vecchio in Florence, built in 1345, is one of the oldest flattened arch bridges in Europe.*

- **The Anji bridge** at Zhao Xian in China was built in 610AD and it is still in use today.

- **Flattened-arch bridges** were first built in Europe in the 14th century. Now they are the norm.

- **London Bridge** was dismantled and reconstructed stone by stone in Arizona as a tourist attraction.

Dams

▲ *The gates of the Thames Barrier in London are designed to shut in times of very high tides to stop seawater rushing up the River Thames and flooding the city.*

- **The earliest known dam** is a 50 ft (15 m) high brick dam on the Nile River at Kosheish in Egypt, built around 2900BC.

- **Two ancient Roman** brick dams, at Proserpina and Cornalbo in southwest Spain, are still in use today.

- **In China** a stone dam was built on the Gukow in 240BC.

- **Masonry dams** today are usually built of concrete blocks as gravity dams, arch dams, or buttress dams.

- **Gravity dams** are very thick dams relying entirely on a huge weight of concrete to hold the water. They are very strong, but costly to build.

- **Arch dams** are built in narrow canyons and curve upstream. Buttress dams are thin dams strengthened by supports called buttresses constructed on the downstream side.

- **Embankment dams** or fill dams are simple dams built from piles of soil, stones, gravel, or clay.

- **The Aswan Dam** on the Nile in Egypt has created Lake Nasser—one of the world's biggest artificial lakes.

- **The world's highest dams** are fill dams in Tajikistan—the Rogun 1,100 ft (335 m) and Nurek 985 ft (300 m). The highest gravity dam is the 935 ft (285 m) Grand Dixence in Switzerland. The highest arch dam is the 892 ft (272 m) Inguri in Georgia.

▶ *Dams can be used to produce electricity. The falling water rotates turbines which are connected to electricity generators.*

FASCINATING FACT
The world's biggest dam is the 837 ft high Kambaratinsk Dam in Russia.

Towns and cities

▲ *São Paulo is one of the world's largest cities in terms of poulation with over 17 million inhabitants.*

- **The first cities** may date from the time when hunters and gatherers settled down to farm 10,000 years ago.

- **The city of Jericho** has been settled for over 10,000 years.

- **One of the oldest** known cities is Catal Hüyük in Anatolia in Turkey, dating from earlier than 6000BC.

- **The first Chinese cities** developed around 1600BC.

- **The cities of Ancient Greece** and Rome were often carefully laid out, with major public buildings. The first known town planner was the Ancient Greek Hippodamus, who planned the city of Miletus.

- **In the 1200s** Paris was by far the biggest city in Europe with a population of around 150,000.

- **In the 1200s,** 320,000 people lived in Hangzhou in China; Guangzhou (Canton) was home to 250,000.

- **In the 1400s** towns like Genoa, Bruges, and Antwerp grew as trading centers. Medieval towns were rarely planned.

- **In the 1800s** huge industrial cities based on factories grew rapidly. Chicago's population jumped from 4,000 in 1840 to 1 million in 1890.

- **The fastest-growing** cities are places like São Paulo in Brazil where many poor people live in quickly erected shanty towns. The world's biggest city is Mexico City.

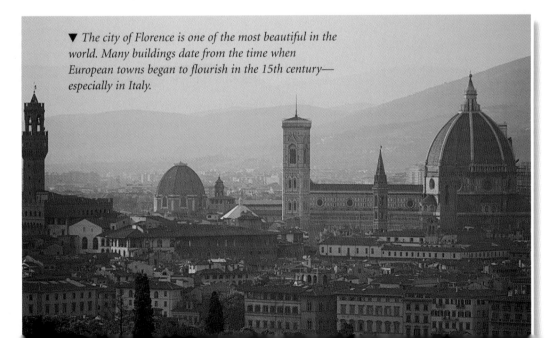

▼ *The city of Florence is one of the most beautiful in the world. Many buildings date from the time when European towns began to flourish in the 15th century—especially in Italy.*

Towers

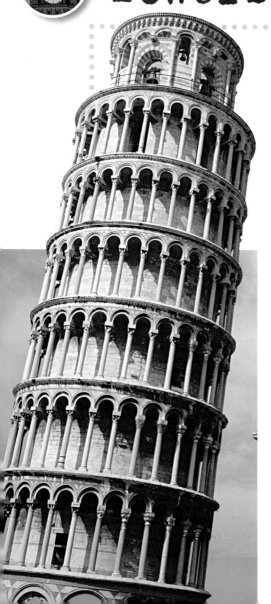

- **Romans, Byzantines,** and medieval Europeans built defensive towers in city walls and beside gates, giving them platforms for raining missiles on enemies.

- **Early churches** had square towers as landmarks to be seen from afar. From the 1100s, European cathedrals had towers called steeples, topped by a pointed spire.

- **Spires began** as pyramids on a tower, but got taller and were tapered to blend into the tower to make a steeple.

- **In the 17th and 18th centuries** church spires became simple and elegant, as in Park Street Church, Boston.

- **The tallest unsupported tower** is Toronto's 1,815 ft- (553 m-) high CN tower.

- **The tallest tower** supported by cables is the 2,065 ft (629 m) TV broadcast tower near Fargo and Blanchard in the U.S.A.

◀ *The Leaning Tower of Pisa in Italy is a 180 ft (55 m) high belltower or "campanile." Building began in 1173, and it started to lean as the workers built the third story. It is now 14.5 ft (4.4 m) out of true.*

- **The Tower of Babel** was a legendary tower built in ancient Babylon in the Near East. The Bible says God didn't want this high tower built, so he made the builders speak different languages to confuse them.

- **The Pharos** was a 443 ft (135 m) lighthouse built c. 283BC to guide ships into the harbor at Alexandria in Egypt.

- **The Tower of Winds** or Horologium, was built in Athens around 100BC to hold a sundial, weather vane, and water clock.

- **Big Ben** is the bell in St. Stephen's Tower in London's Houses of Parliament. The tower once had a cell where "rioters" like suffragette Emmeline Pankhurst were held.

◀ *Big Ben first tolled in 1859.*

115

The first houses

▲ *Roman villas had colonnaded corridors, gardens, and pools.*

- **It was once thought** that all prehistoric humans lived in caves, but caves were mostly used for religious rituals. The earliest houses were made of materials like wood, leaves, grass, and mud—so all traces have now vanished.

- **Stone Age people** probably lived in round huts, with walls of wooden posts and thatches of reed.

- **In Britain,** post-holes and hearths have been found dating back 10,000 years in places like London's Hampstead Heath and Broom Hill in Hampshire.

- **Early mudbrick** houses dating from at least 9,500 years ago are found in Anatolia in the Middle East.

- **Low walls** of big stones were the base for thatched roofs 6,500 years ago at places like Carn Brea in Cornwall.

- **Two-story houses** in Mohenjo Daro in Pakistan from 5,000 years ago were built from sun-dried mud bricks and boasted courtyards, doors, windows, and bathrooms.

- **Big ancient Egyptian** houses had three main areas—a reception room for business, a hall in the center for guests, and private quarters at the back for family members.

- **Tomb models** show how Egyptian homes looked.

- **Big Roman country houses** were called villas; a town house was known as a domus.

- **Villas** had tiled roofs, verandahs, heating, marbled floors, lavishly decorated walls and bathrooms.

▶ *Some home-building styles have changed little in thousands of years. These stilt houses are in French Polynesia.*

Chinese buildings

- **China** developed its own distinctive style of building over 3,000 years ago.

- **Traditionally, large Chinese buildings** were made of wood on a stone base.

- **A distinctive feature** is a large tiled overhanging roof, ending in a graceful upturn. The tiles were glazed blue, green, or yellow.

- **The roof** is supported not by the walls but by wooden columns, often carved and painted red and gold.

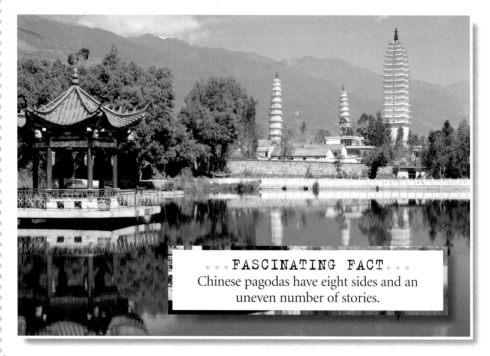

FASCINATING FACT
Chinese pagodas have eight sides and an uneven number of stories.

▲ *Pagodas in Dali, China. The ground story of a pagoda may contain shrines and images.*

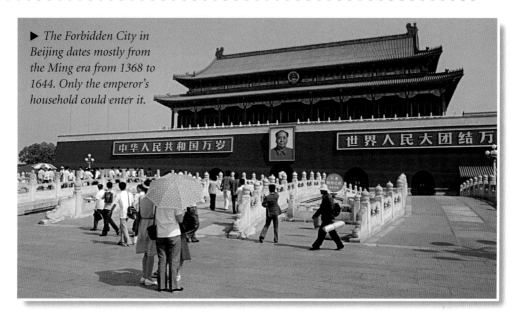

▶ *The Forbidden City in Beijing dates mostly from the Ming era from 1368 to 1644. Only the emperor's household could enter it.*

- **Walls were thin** and simply gave privacy and warmth.

- **Chinese temples** were constructed as large wooden halls with elaborate roof beams in the ceiling.

- **Pagodas** are tall tapering towers often linked to Buddhist temples. They have from 3 to 15 stories.

- **In China, pagodas** were believed to bring happiness to the surrounding community. They were made of wood, bricks, tiles, or even porcelain and decorated with ivory.

- **Pagodas** came from India and developed from Buddhist burial mounds called stupas.

Modern architecture

◀ Old and new in Hong Kong: the modern Hong Kong-Shanghai Bank dwarfs a 19th-century classical building.

- **In the 1920s** many architects rejected old styles to experiment with simple shapes in materials like glass, steel, and concrete.

- **The International Style** was pioneered by the Swiss architect Le Corbusier who built houses in smooth geometric shapes like boxes.

- **The Bauhaus** school in Germany believed buildings should look like the job they were meant to do.

- **Walter Gropius** and Mies van de Rohe brought Bauhaus ideas to the U.S.A. and developed sleek, glass-walled, steel-framed skyscrapers like New York's Seagram Building.

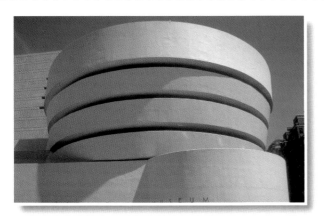

◀ *The Guggenheim Museum, New York City. This unique circular building was designed by Frank Lloyd Wright.*

- **American Frank Lloyd Wright** (1869–1959) was famous both for his low, prairie-style bungalows "growing" from their site and his airy and elegant geometric buildings.

- **In the 1950s** architects like Kenzo Tange of Japan reacted against the "blandness" of the International Style, introducing a rough concrete look called Brutalism.

- **In the 1960s** many critics reacted against the damage done by modern architecture to historic cities.

- **Post-modernists** were united in rejecting modern architecture, often reviving historical styles. American Robert Venturi added traditional decoration.

- **Richard Rogers' and Renzo Piano's** Pompidou Center in Paris (1977) was a humorous joke on the Bauhaus idea, exposing the "bones" of the building.

- **With shiny metal** and varied shapes the Guggenheim Gallery in Bilbao in Spain is a new masterpiece.

Mosques

- **The word "mosque"** comes from the Arabic term masjid, which means a place of kneeling.

- **Mosques** are places where Muslims worship. Muslims can worship anywhere clean. So a mosque can be just a stick in the sand to mark out a space for 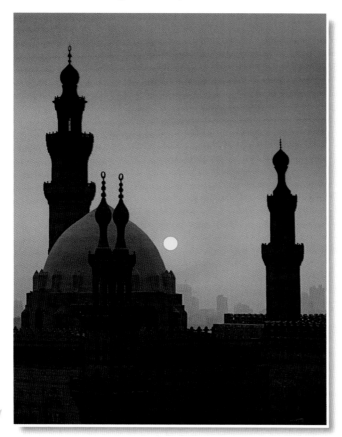 praying or even just a mat. But many mosques are beautiful buildings.

- **Cathedral or Friday** mosques are large mosques big enough to hold all the adult Muslims in the area.

- **Typically** mosques have a courtyard surrounded by four walls called iwans. There is often a fountain or fuawara at the center for ceremonial washing.

◀ *Typically, minarets on mosques have onion-shaped roofs.*

- **The mihrab** is a decorative niche on the inner wall closest to the city of Mecca that Muslims face when praying.

- **The mimbar** is the stone or wooden pulpit where the Imam, the chief officer in the mosque, leads the people in prayer.

- **Most mosques** have two to six tall pointed towers which are called minarets.

- **On each minaret** is a balcony from which muezzin (criers) call the faithful to prayer five times a day.

- **Minarets** may have been inspired by the Pharos, the famous lighthouse at Alexandria in Egypt.

- **There are** no paintings or statues in mosques, only abstract patterns, often made of tiles.

◀ *The Great Hassan II Mosque in Casablanca, Morocco, was completed in 1993. It has the tallest minaret of any Islamic mosque. It is 656 ft (200 m) high.*

123

The Colosseum

▲ *The Colosseum in Rome was one of the greatest buildings of the ancient world.*

- **The Colosseum** was a huge stone sports arena built in ancient Rome.

- **It was 620 ft (189 m) long**, 510 ft (156 m) wide, and 170 ft (52 m) high.

- **It held** about 50,000 spectators who entered through 80 entrances.

- **The sports** included fights between gladiators with swords, nets, and other weapons who fought to the death. They also fought against lions and other wild beasts.

- **Counterweighted** doors allowed 64 wild beasts to be released from their cages simultaneously.

- **It took just eight years**—from around AD70 to AD78—to build the entire structure of the Colosseum.

- **To build** it the Romans brought almost a quarter of a million tons of stone by barge from quarries 12 mi (20 km) outside Rome.

- **During construction,** a cart carrying a ton of stone would leave the riverside wharves every seven minutes on the 1 mi (1.5 km) journey to the site.

- **A huge awning** called a velarium, supported by 240 masts, protected the arena from bad weather.

- **Its opening was celebrated** by spectacular games lasting 100 days.

▼ *Romans admired gladiators for their strength, bravery, and skill. However, their lives were short and their deaths were horrible.*

St. Sophia

- **Saint or Hagia Sophia** was built as a Christian cathedral in Istanbul in Turkey (Roman "Byzantium").

- **Hagia Sophia** is Greek for "holy wisdom."

- **St. Sophia** was built between 532 and 537AD, when Istanbul was called Constantinople.

- **The great Byzantine** emperor Justinian I ordered the building of St. Sophia after a fire destroyed an earlier church on the site.

- **St. Sophia** was designed by the brilliant Byzantine architects Anthemius of Tralles and Isidorus of Miletus.

- **The main structure** is a framework of arches and vaults (high arched ceilings).

- **The dome** is 102 ft (31 m) across and 184 ft (56 m) high. It is supported by four triangular brick pillars called pendentives.

- **St. Sophia is decorated** with marble veneers and mosaics of Mary, Christ, angels, and bishops.

- **In 1453** the Ottoman Turks took the city and converted St. Sophia to a mosque. They plastered over the mosaics and added four minarets on the outside.

- **In 1935** St. Sophia was converted into a museum and the mosaics were uncovered.

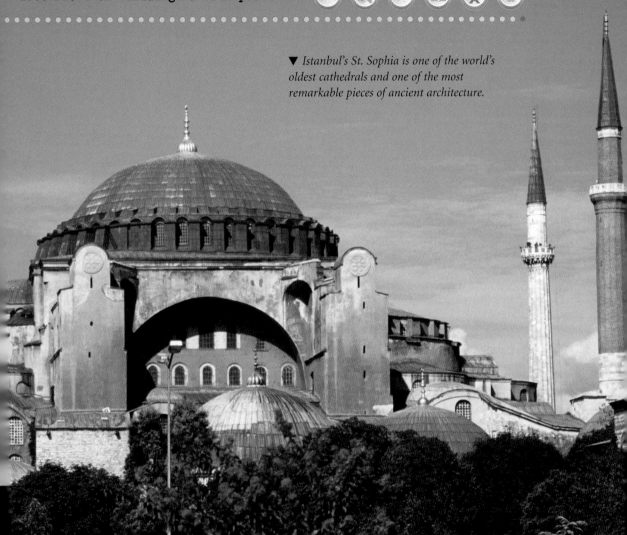

▼ *Istanbul's St. Sophia is one of the world's oldest cathedrals and one of the most remarkable pieces of ancient architecture.*

Golden Gate Bridge

▼ *San Francisco's Golden Gate Bridge is one of the most beautiful, and busiest, bridges in the world.*

- **The Golden Gate Bridge** spans the entrance to San Francisco Bay in California.

- **The Golden Gate Bridge** is one of the world's largest suspension bridges.

- **The total length** of the bridge is 8,980 ft (2,737 m).

- **The towers at either end** are 1,115 ft (340 m) high. The suspended span between the towers is 4,200 ft (1,280 m), one of the longest in the world.

- **The roadway** is 220 ft (67 m) above the water, although this varies according to the height of the tide

> **...FASCINATING FACT...**
> The tower's foundations are being
> reinforced to withstand earthquakes.

- **The Golden Gate Bridge** was designed by Joseph Baerman Strauss and built for $35 million, a third of the original cost estimate.

- **The bridge was opened** to traffic on May 27, 1937.

- **The bridge carries** two six-lane highways and pedestrian paths.

- **Unusually, the bridge** is double-deck, carrying traffic one way on the upper deck and the other way on the lower deck.

Stonehenge

- **Stonehenge** is an ancient stone monument in southern England made from circles of huge rough-cut stones.

- **The main circle of stones** or "sarsens" is a ring of 30 huge upright stones, joined at the top by 30 lintels. Many of these sarsens have now fallen or been looted and used to make bridges and dams.

- **Inside the sarsen** ring are five "doorways" called trilithons, each made with three gigantic stones, weighing up to 40 tons each.

- **In between** are rings of smaller bluestones.

- **The bluestones** come from the Preseli Hills in Wales, 150 mi (240 km) away. Archeologists puzzle over how they were carried here.

- **At the center** is a single tall stone, called the Heel Stone.

- **Stonehenge was built** in three phases between 2950BC and 1600BC, starting with just a huge earth ring.

▼ *Experiments have shown a team of 150 people could haul the stones upright, but dragging them to the site on greased wooden sleds must have been a huge undertaking.*

▲ *The base of each upright stone was placed over a post-hole. Ropes and timber scaffolding were then used to raise the stones into an upright position.*

- **Archeologists** believe it was a gathering place and a site for religious ceremonies for Bronze Age people.

- **Newman, Thom, and Hawkins** have shown the layout of the stones ties in with astronomical events.

- **At sunrise on midsummer's day** (the solstice), the sun shines directly along the avenue to the Heel Stone.

Theaters

- **In the days of ancient Greece and Rome** thousands of people went to see dramas in huge, stone-built open-air theaters like sports arenas.

- **The Wooden Os** which appeared in England around 1570 were the first real theaters since Roman times. They were round wooden buildings with the stage and audience arena in the middle, open to the sky.

- **The 17th century** was the "Golden Age" of drama in Spain.

- **In the 17th century** theater moved indoors for the first time. Performances were by candlelight in large halls with rows of balconies around the edge.

- **In early theaters** the actors mostly performed on a bare stage. Toward the end of the 18th century, cut-out boards with realistic scenes painted on them were slid in from the wings (the sides of the stage).

- **In the early 19th century** theaters grew much bigger to cater for the populations of the new industrial cities, often holding thousands. Huge stages were illuminated by "limelight"—brightly burning pellets of calcium.

- **Most of the grand old** theaters we can visit today date from the mid-1800s.

- **The big theaters** of the early 19th century had huge backstage areas with lots of room for "flying in" scenery, and also spring-loaded trapdoors and other ingenious mechanisms for creating giant special effects, like exploding volcanoes and runaway trains.

- **Toward the end of the 19th century** dedicated amateurs, fed up with special effects, performed in smaller spaces, such as clubs, barns, and private houses. These developed into intimate "studio" theaters where actors could stage subtle, realistic plays.

- **Many modern theaters** are equipped with very bright, computer-controlled lighting, sound systems, and motorized stage machinery.

132

▶ *There were several "Wooden O" theaters like this in Elizabethan London in the late 16th century—including the famous Globe where Shakespeare first staged many of his plays.*

Entrance where the audience lined up for the mid-afternoon performances

Walls made from plaster and wood

Rowdy audience pit where poorer people stood

Bare stage where actors performed

Balconies where lords and ladies sat

133

The Tower of London

- **The Tower of London** is the oldest stone castle in London, started by William the Conqueror after his conquest of England in 1066. The Crown Jewels are kept here.

- **The oldest part of the Tower** is the great square keep called the White Tower which dates from 1078.

- **The Tower** later gained two surrounding "curtain" walls, like other castles.

- **The inner curtain** wall has 13 towers, including the Bloody Tower, Beauchamp Tower, and Wakefield Tower.

- **Traitors' Gate** is an arch beside the River Thames. It gets its name from the time when high-ranking traitors were ferried here by boat to be imprisoned in the Tower. They entered this way.

- **Many people** have been imprisoned here like Princess (later Queen) Elizabeth and her mother Anne Boleyn in the 1500s.

▲ *Guy Fawkes and his fellow conspirators were imprisoned in the Tower of London.*

▲ *The Tower of London is the most famous medieval castle in Britain.*

- **Little Ease** is a dark 35 sq ft (3.3 sq m) cell where prisoners could neither stand up nor lie down.
- **Many prisoners were** beheaded here, including Sir Thomas More and Sir Walter Raleigh.
- **In 1483** the boy king Edward V and his young brother were thought to have been murdered here. Bones which could have been theirs were later found under stairs.
- **Yeoman Warders** are the Tower's special guards. They are nicknamed beefeaters. The name may have come from a fondness for roast beef or the French word *buffetier*.

Greek and Roman buildings

▲ *The most famous Greek temple is the Parthenon in Athens, built c 450BC.*

- **Ancient Greek and Roman** architecture are together known as Classical architecture.

- **The key features** of Classical buildings are solid, elegantly plain geometric shapes including pillars, arches, and friezes.

- **The main Greek** building was the temple with its triangular roof of pale stone on rows of tall columns.

- **Greek temples** were designed in mathematical ratios.

- **Roman architect** Vitruvius described three orders (styles) of columns: Doric, Ionic, and Corinthian.

- **Each order** has its own character: Doric serious and strong, Ionic graceful, and Corinthian rich and festive.

- **The Parthenon** is a Doric temple built by architects Ictinus and Callicrates guided by the sculptor Phidias.

- **Roman buildings** used many arches and vaults (ceilings made from arches joined together).

- **The ruined Baths of Caracalla** in Rome (AD217) has huge and graceful vaults.

- **Classical** architecture has inspired many imitations over the centuries, including the Palladian style of the 1600s.

▶ *Ornate Corinthian columns would have been seen on Roman temples.*

The Statue of Liberty

- **New York's Statue of Liberty** stands on Liberty Island off the tip of Manhattan.

- **The statue** was dedicated on October 28, 1886 by President Cleveland.

- **It was paid for** by the French people to celebrate their friendship with the U.S.A.

- **Sculptor** Frédéric-Auguste Bartholdi began work on the statue in Paris in 1875.

- **It was built** from 452 copper sheets hammered into shape by hand and mounted on four huge steel supports designed by Eiffel and Viollet-le-Duc.

- **The 225 ton statue** was shipped to New York in 1885.

▲ *The Statue of Liberty towers above Liberty Island at the entrance to New York Harbor.*

- **A pedestal** designed by Richard Hunt and paid for by 121,000 Americans brought it to a total height of 305 ft (93 m).

- **The statue's full name** is *Liberty Enlightening the World.* The seven spikes in the crown stand for Liberty's light shining on the world's seven seas and continents. The tablet in Her left hand is America's Declaration of Independence.

- **Emma Lazarus's sonnet** *The New Colossus* on the pedestal ends: "Give me your tired poor, your huddled masses of your teeming shore. Send these, the homeless, tempest-tossed to me. I lift my lamp beside the golden door!"

▲ New York's famous statue of Liberty, before it was restored in 1986 and the flame covered in gold leaf.

139

St. Basil's Cathedral

▲ *Religious paintings adorn the interiors of Russian churches, like this one from St. Basil's Cathedral.*

- **The cathedral of** St. Basil the Blessed in Moscow's Red Square was built from 1554 to 1560.

- **St. Basil's** is made up of ten tower churches: the biggest is 150 ft (46 m) tall.

- **It began with** eight little wooden churches: each built between 1552 and 1554 after a major Russian victory against the Tartars of Kazan.

- **After the final victory** Ivan the Terrible ordered stone churches to be built in place of the wooden ones.

- **Legend says** each of the onion-shaped domes represents the turban of a defeated Tartar lord.

- **St. Basil's** may have been designed by two Russians: Posnik and Barma. Records are unclear and they may have been one person.

- **Legend says** the Italian builder was blinded afterward so he could build nothing like it again.

- **Originally** it was known as the Cathedral of the Intercession, but in 1588 a tenth church was added in honor of St. Basil and it was known afterward as St. Basil's.

- **Napoleon and Stalin** both tried to destroy the cathedral.

- **In 1955** restorers found the secret of the cathedral's construction embedded in the brickwork—wooden models used as silhouettes to guide the builders.

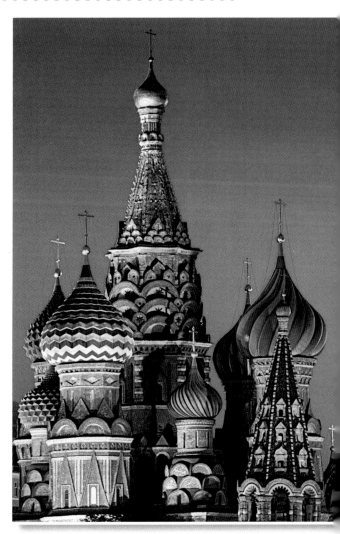

▶ *With its ten famous colorful towers, St. Basil's in Moscow is like no other Christian cathedral in the world.*

St. Paul's Cathedral

▲ *The ceiling of the choir in St. Paul's Cathedral is adorned with mosaic-work.*

- **The present St. Paul's** cathedral in London is the fifth church on the site.

- **On the same site** in Roman times, there was a temple dedicated to Diana.

- **The first St. Paul's** was built of wood in AD604 by St. Ethelbert, King of Kent.

- **The Norman cathedral** was started around 1090 by Maurice, chaplain to William the Conqueror.

- **The Norman cathedral** called "Old St. Paul's" had the highest spire ever built, but it was struck down by lightning in 1561.

- **The first public lottery** was held in Old St. Paul's in 1569 to raise money for repairs. The churchyard was famous for its booksellers, like Wynkyn de Worde in the 1400s.

- **Old St. Paul's** burned to the ground in the Great Fire of London in 1666.

- **The new St. Paul's** was designed by Sir Christopher Wren, the architect of many other London buildings. Wren thought the 365 ft- (111 m-) high dome he wanted to be seen from the outside was too lofty for the inside. So inside the outer dome, he built another 65 ft (20 m) lower. Work began in 1675 and was completed in 1711.

- **If you whisper** inside the dome's famous "whispering gallery" you can be heard on the far side 115ft (35m) away.

- **Among the famous tombs** in the crypt of St. Paul's are those of Admiral Nelson and the Duke of Wellington.

▶ *St. Paul's is one of the world's largest and most elegant cathedrals. It was built in the classical (Roman) style by the great architect Christopher Wren in the 17th century.*

Palaces

▲ *London's Buckingham Palace is the home of the Queen of the United Kingdom.*

- **The palaces** of Europe owe much to the vast palaces of the caliphs of the Near East, built in 7th and 8th centuries, with their cool courtyards and rich decoration.

- **The Topkapi Palace** in Istanbul was the sumptuous home of the Ottoman sultans for over 400 years until it was made into a museum in 1924, after the sultans' fall.

- **Venice's Doge's Palace** (mainly 1400s) shows oriental touches brought from the east by Venetian merchants.

- **The elegant Pitti Palace** in Florence was designed by the brilliant architect Brunelleschi for the merchant Luca Pitti in 1440. It was taken over by the Medici family in 1550.

- **Hampton Court Palace** southwest of London was begun in 1514 by King Henry VIII's favorite, Cardinal Wolsey—but when Wolsey fell from favor, the King took it over.

- **The Escorial** in Madrid is a massive granite palace built by Philip II. It was begun in 1563 and completed in 1584.

- **Many 18th-century princes** built their own lavish palaces like those at Dresden and Potsdam in Germany, Vienna's Schönbrunn, and the Winter Palace in St. Petersburg.

- **Buckingham House** in London was built in 1702–5 for the Duke of Buckingham but remodeled as a palace in 1825.

- **Peter the Great** made Russia's oldest garden, the Summer Garden at St. Petersburg, in 1710. He built the Summer Palace in it.

- **Catherine the Great** had the St. Petersburg's Winter Palace built by architect Bartolomeo Rastrelli in 1762.

▲ From the 1760s the Winter Palace, St. Petersburg, was the main residence of the Russian Tsars.

Ancient palaces

▲ *The Potala palace has thirteen floors and over 1,000 rooms.*

- **The word palace** comes from the Palatine Hill in Rome, where the emperors of Rome had their palaces.

- **The earliest known** palaces are those built in Thebes in Ancient Egypt by King Thutmose III in the 15th century BC.

- **Egyptian palaces** had a rectangular wall enclosing a maze of small rooms and a courtyard—a pattern later followed by many Asian palaces.

- **The Babylonians** and Persians introduced grand halls in their palaces at Susa and elsewhere.

- **Minoan palaces** on Crete introduced extra stories.

- **Roman palaces** were the grandest of the ancient world.

- **The Sacred Palace** of Byzantium (now Istanbul) was biggest of all, covering 3,595,000 sq ft (334,000 sq m).

- **Palaces** in China and Japan, like Beijing's Forbidden City, often had a high wall surrounding small houses for the ruler and his officials.

- **Ancient palaces in the Americas,** like the Mayan palace at Uxmal dating from AD900, are usually simpler.

- **Potala palace** stands high above Lhasa in Tibet. Potala means "high heavenly realm." The original, built by King Srong-brtsan-sgam-po in the 7th century, was destroyed by the Chinese c.1600. The Dalai Lama rebuilt it in 1645.

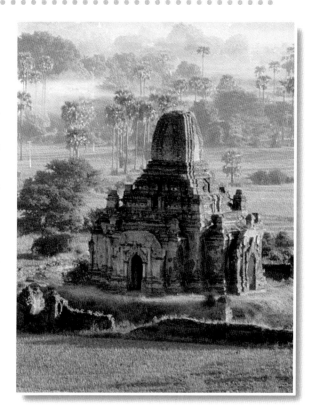

▲ *The 12th-century Khmer emperors of Cambodia built magnificent palaces in their capital of Angkor, now overgrown by jungle. But most magnificent of all was the temple, Angkor Wat.*

147

The Palace of Versailles

▲ *Versailles is perhaps the most expensive palace ever built.*

- **Versailles**, in France, is a magnificent palace built for Louis XIV. Work began in 1661 and carried on for a century.

- **When complete** Versailles was 1,640 ft (500 m) long, had over 1,300 major rooms, and could accommodate 5,000 people.

- **The first architect** was Louis le Vau but Jules Hardouin-Mansart took over in 1676, adding the second story.

- **The interior** was conceived by Charles le Brun. His Hall of Mirrors is a long hall lined with mirrors. A masterly painted ceiling shows Louis XIV's achievements.

- **Throughout Versailles** high ceilings and great doors are emblazoned in gold with the mark of the sun god, Apollo—and also that of King Louis, known as the Sun King.

- **The huge gardens** of tree-lined terraces and ponds were landscaped by Andre le Notre with 1,400 fountains, 400 new pieces of sculpture, and four million tulips.

- **The fountains** appear "magically" still to show the power of the king over nature.

- **The palace** had a famous state-of-the-art theater designed by Jacques-Ange Gabriel in 1769.

- **During the French Revolution** on October 6, 1789, mobs invaded the palace and wrecked its interiors. Restoration began in 1837 and has continued ever since.

- **The avenues of Washington DC** were laid out in imitation of Versailles by a French architect.

▶ *The gardens at Versailles have been enlarged several times and now cover nearly 250 acres (101 hectares). Plantings, fountains, and statues are arranged in geometric patterns.*

Pyramids

- **Pyramids** are huge ancient monuments with a square base and triangular sides coming together in a point at the top. Remarkably, they are found not only in Egypt, but also in Greece, Cyprus, Italy, India, Thailand, Mexico, South America, and various Pacific islands.

- **The earliest tombs** of the pharaohs were mud chambers called mastabas. But c.2686BC, the architect Imhotep had a pyramid-shaped tomb built for Zoser at Saqqara. This rose in steps and so is called the Step Pyramid.

- **In 2600BC** the Egyptians filled in the steps on a pyramid with stones to make the first smooth pyramid at Medum.

- **The ruins of 80 pyramids** stand near the Nile in Egypt, built over 1,000 years. Each has an elaborate system of hidden passageways and chambers to stop robbers getting at the tomb of the pharaoh inside.

- **The largest pyramid** is the Great Pyramid at Giza, built for the Pharaoh Khufu c.2551–2472BC. This was once 482 ft (147 m) high, but is now 460 ft (140 m), since some upper stones have been lost. Khufu is known as Cheops in Greek.

- **Later the Egyptians** abandoned pyramids and cut tombs into rock, as in the Valley of Kings at Thebes. The tomb of Tutankhamun was one of these.

- **The Moche Indians** of Peru built large brick pyramids, including the Pyramid of the Sun near Trujillo.

- **Another Pyramid of the Sun** is on the site of the ancient Aztec capital of Teotihuacan, 30 mi (50 km) from Mexico City. Built around 2,000 years ago it is exactly the same size 2,475 sq ft (230 sq m) as the Great Pyramid at Giza.

- **The American pyramids** were not tombs like those in Egypt, but temples, so they have no hidden chambers inside. They are built not from blocks of cut stone but from millions of basketloads of volcanic ash and gravel.

▲ *The strange half-lion, half-pharaoh
statue called the Sphinx stands near the
pyramid of Pharaoh Khafre at Giza.*

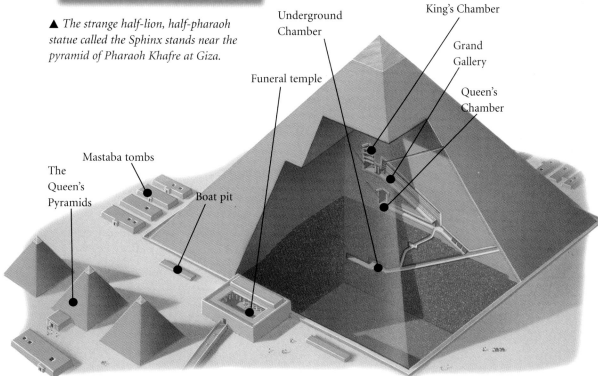

Underground
Chamber

King's Chamber

Grand
Gallery

Queen's
Chamber

Funeral temple

Mastaba tombs

The
Queen's
Pyramids

Boat pit

151

The Taj Mahal

- **The Taj Mahal** (said tarj m'hal) in Agra in India is perhaps the most beautiful tomb in the world.

- **Mughal Indian** ruler Shah Jehan ordered it to be built in honor of his favorite wife Mumtaz Mahal, who died giving birth to their 14th child.

- **Mumtaz** died in 1629, and the Taj was built over 22 years from 1632 to 1653.

- **The Taj** is set at the north end of a formal Persian garden with water courses and rows of cypress trees.

- **It is made of white** marble and sits on a platform of sandstone.

- **Inside** behind an octagonal screen of alabaster marble tracery lie the jewel-inlaid cenotaphs (tombs) of Mumtaz and Shah Jehan. The Shah was placed there when he died and his tomb is the only asymmetrical feature in the Taj.

- **20,000 worker**s worked in marble and sandstone, silver, gold, carnelian, jasper, moonstone, jade, lapis lazuli, and coral to enhance the Taj's beauty.

- **At each corner** of the platform is a slender minaret 133 ft (40.5 m) tall.

- **In the center** is a dome 70 ft (21.3 m) across and 120 ft (36.6 m) high.

- **The main architect** was Iranian Isa Khan, but the decorations were said to be by Austin of Bordeaux and Veroneo of Venice.

◀ *So perfect are the Taj's proportions that it was said to have been designed by giants and finished by jewelers.*

153

Ancient America

▲ *The Aztecs built great pyramid-temples in their capital, Tenochtitlan, which lay on a series of lakes in central Mexico. Their many gods included gods of the Sun, rain, and wind, to whom they made human sacrifices.*

- **The largest buildings** in ancient America were Mayan pyramids, like the Tomb of Pakal in South Mexico.

- **Tenochtitlan** in Mexico is one of the best preserved ancient cities in the world, with its magnificent pyramids, palaces, temples, courts, and homes.

- **At its height**, around 2,000 years ago, Tenochtitlan was the world's biggest city with 100,000 people.

- **Hopewell Indians** of Newark, Ohio built earthwork tombs in AD250 that rivaled the size of Egypt's pyramids.

- **Aztecs** built the Great Temple pyramid in their ancient capital of Tenochtitlan (now Mexico City) from 1325–1500. Human sacrifices were made at the top.

- **The Mesa Verde** is a famous "pueblo" (stone village) of the Anasazi in New Mexico, abandoned around AD1100.

- **In the Chaco Canyon** the Anasazi built 400 mi (650 km) of mysterious roads that lead to nowhere.

- **Nazca Lines are** huge outlines of birds, monkeys, and other things up to 325 ft (100 m) across, drawn by Nazca people in the desert in southern Peru. They date from c.100BC to AD700.

- **The Nazca Lines** are only clearly seen from the air. They may have been part of a giant astronomical calendar.

> ...FASCINATING FACT...
> The Incas of Peru built 15,500 mi of
> stone-paved roads between 1450 and 1532.

▶ *The 1,500 year-old pyramids of the Maya were once overgrown by jungle, but most have now been revealed.*

155

The Eiffel Tower

- **The Eiffel Tower** in Paris was 1,025 ft (312.2 m) high when it was first built. An antenna brings it up to 1,045 ft (318.7 m). There are 1,665 steps up to the top.

- **On a clear day** you can see 50 mi (80 km) in all directions from the top. It is often sunny at the top when the weather in the Paris streets is cloudy.

- **The tower was made** from 18,038 pieces of iron, held together by 2,500,000 rivets.

- **It was built in 1889** for the exhibition celebrating the 100th anniversary of the French Revolution.

▶ *Paris' Eiffel Tower is one of the world's most famous landmarks.*

- **Gustave Eiffel** (1832–1923) was the most successful engineer of the day, building not only the Eiffel Tower but New York's Statue of Liberty too.

- **The Eiffel Tower** was designed by Maurice Koechlin and Emile Nougier who calculated the effects of wind and gravity with amazing precision.

- **The Tower** was intended to show what could be done with cast iron.

- **During building work** Parisian artists, such as the composer Gounod and the poet Maupassant, protested against its ugliness. But when completed it was an instant success with ordinary people.

- **The cost of building** the Eiffel Tower was over $1 million. However, the fees from the visitors in the first year alone covered the construction costs.

- **When Paris was occupied** by the Nazis during the war, the elevators "mysteriously" stopped working. They restarted the day Paris was liberated.

▶ *Approximately two million people visited the Eiffel Tower in the first year it was open.*

Sydney Opera House

- **Sydney Opera House** in Sydney, opened in October 1973, is one of Australia's best-known landmarks.

- **The design** by Danish architect Jorn Utzon was agreed after a competition involving 233 entries, but it took 14 years to build.

- **The radical sail-like** roofs were said to have been inspired by sea shells.

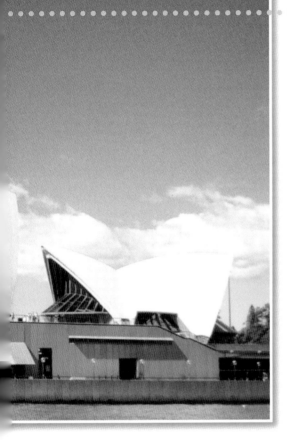

▲ *Standing by the water's edge in Sydney Harbor, Sydney Opera House is one of the world's most distinctive buildings.*

- **The original design** was so unusual that it proved impossible to build structurally, so Utzon altered the shape of the roofs to base them on sections of a ball.

- **The altered design** meant the roofs could be made from pre-cast concrete slabs.

- **The roofs** were made from 2,194 pre-cast concrete slabs, weighing up to 15 tons each.

- **The slabs** are tied together with 220 mi (350 km) of tensioned steel cable and covered with one million Swedish tiles.

- **In the mouths of the roofs** are 67,000 sq ft (6,225 sq m) of double layered French glass. One layer of each pair is tinted a topaz color.

- **Inside** there were originally four theaters: the Concert Hall, the Opera Theater, the Drama Theater, and the Playhouse.

- **A new theater,** The Studio, was added in March 1999 for small cast plays and films.

Early boats

◀ ▲ *Outriggers (above) were used to colonize the Pacific tens of thousands of years ago. But many early boats like the Welsh coracle (left) were made by stretching animal skins over a wooden frame.*

- **The Aborigines** arrived by boat in Australia at least 50,000 years ago, as cave paintings show.

- **The oldest remains** of boats are 8,000 or so years old, like the 13 ft (4 m) canoe found at Pesse in Holland.

- **Many early canoes** were simply hollowed out logs, called dugouts.

- **The islands of the Pacific** were probably colonized by dugouts, stabilized by attaching an outrigger (an extra float on the side) or adding extra hulls.

- **Lighter canoes** could be made by stretching animal skins over a light frame of bent wood.

- **4,000 years ago,** Ancient Egyptians were constructing ships over 100 ft (30 m) long by interlocking planks of wood and lashing them together with grass rope.

- **By 1000BC,** Phoenician traders were sailing into the Atlantic in ships made of planks of Cedar trees.

- **All early boats** were driven by hand, using either a pole pushed along the bottom, or a paddle.

- **Sails** were used for the first time 7,000 years ago in Mesopotamia on reed trading boats.

- **The first known picture** of a sail is 5,500 years old and comes from Egypt.

▶ *Ancient stories suggest that thousands of years ago the Polynesians sailed in large, twin-hulled canoes.*

Viking longships

◀ *The longship's longer keel and tapered ends made it more seaworthy and faster than earlier ships.*

- **Viking longships** were the long narrow boats built by the Viking warriors of Scandinavia around AD1000.

- **A virtually** intact ship was found in 1880 at Gokstad near Oseberg in Norway. A king was buried inside it.

- **Longships** were very fast, light, and seaworthy. They carried the Viking explorer Leif Ericsson all the way across the Atlantic to North America.

- **In 1893** a replica of the Gokstad ship sailed across the Atlantic in 28 days.

- **Some Viking longships** were up to 100 ft (30 m) long and 55 ft (17 m) across and could carry 200 warriors.

- **At sea** longships relied on a single, large square sail made up from strips of woolen cloth; on rivers and in calm they used oar-power, with 20 to 30 rowers on each side.

- **The special design of their ships** allowed the Vikings to make raids far up shallow rivers.

- **The prow curved** up to a carved dragon head.

- **Longships** were for carrying warriors on raids, but the Vikings also built wider, deeper "knarrs" for trade and small rowing boats called "faerings."

- **The Viking** ships were very stable because they had a keel, a wooden board about 55 ft (17 m) long and 18 in (45 cm) deep, along the bottom of the boat.

▶ *Viking warriors believed that a heroic death would bring them glory and a place in Valhalla, home of the Norse gods.*

Dhows

▶ *Dhows like this are still built today in Lamu in Africa, much as they were 1,000 or more years ago.*

- **Dhows** are wooden Arab boats that have been used in the waters of the Mediterranean and Indian Ocean for thousands of years.

- **Most dhows** are now made of teak (or Glass Reinforced Plastic). In the past, mango wood was common.

- **In the past** dhows were made, not by nailing planks of wood together, but by sewing them with coconut fiber.

- **Dhow builders** rarely use plans. They judge entirely by eye and experience.

- **Dhows traditionally** had lateen sails—triangular sails in line with the boat. This allows them to sail almost into the wind.

- **Although many dhows** are now motorized, they usually have a tall manual mast for unloading.

- **There are several kinds** of dhow, including the shu'ai, the boum, the sambuq, the jelbut, and the ghanjah.

- **The jelbut** is thought to get its name from the English "jolly boat"—the little boats visiting British East Indiamen sent ashore. Jelbuts were often used for pearl fishing. Racing jelbuts have a treetrunk-like bowsprit almost as long as the hull to carry extra sails.

- **Sambuqs and ghanjahs** are thought to get their square sterns from 17th-century Portuguese galleons.

- **Boums** can be up to 400 tons and 165 ft (50 m) long.

▼ *The building, repairing, and sailing of dhows is still a common sight in the United Arab Emirates.*

Junks

- **Junks** are wooden sailing boats that have been used in China and the Far East for thousands of years.

  - **Typical junks** have a broad flat bow (front).

    - **Typical junks** have a broad, high stern castle (rear).

      - **Junks have lugsails.** These are triangular sails arranged almost in line with the boat, allowing the boat to sail almost into the wind—unlike the square sails of early European boats which only worked with the wind behind.

◄ *Most sailing junks have two or three masts. Some have more. The sails are made from cotton and supported by bamboo struts.*

- **The Chinese** are believed to have invented lugsails.

- **By the 1400s** the Chinese were building junks 490 ft (150 m) long and almost 330 ft (100 m) wide—bigger than any sailing ship yet built in Europe.

- **In 1405** the Chinese admiral Cheng Ho led a fleet of exploration through the Indian Ocean. His fleet consisted of 62 large junks and 255 small junks. Each of the large junks was gigantic compared with Columbus's *Santa Maria*. The biggest junk was over 1,500 tons—the *Santa Maria* was only 98 tons.

- **Between 1790 and 1810** traders in the South Seas were terrorized by vast fleets of pirate junks, led by the female pirate Cheng I Sao.

- **Nowadays** most junks are motorized.

- **Junks** are often moored permanently as homes.

▼ *With their huge fleets of pirate junks, Chinese pirates wielded great power on the seas.*

167

Galleons

▲ *The Spanish Armada was defeated by English ships in the battle of Gravelines in 1588, off the coast of France.*

- **Galleons** were huge sailing ships, built from the mid 1500s onward.

- **Galleons** had tall structures called castles at either end.

- **The front castle** was called the forecastle or fo'c'sle (said folk-sel).

- **The rear castle** was called the stern castle and it housed elaborate living quarters for the officers. The crew lived in crowded rows below deck.

- **The stern of the ship** was often ornately carved, decorated with gold, and painted bright colors.

- **A galleon** had three tall masts: the foremast, the mainmast, and the mizzenmast at the rear.

168

- **Galleons** were both warships and trading boats and carried large numbers of cannon and troops.

- **In the 1500s** a number of Spanish galleons crossed the Atlantic carrying gold from the Americas to Spain.

- **When the Spanish Armada** of galleons was sent to attack England in 1588, they were defeated by the smaller English ships which were faster and lighter despite their heavy armament.

▶ *Spanish galleons were targets for pirates, as they carried huge amounts of treasure. Pirates used ships called galleys, which were smaller, faster, and able to outmaneuver the huge Spanish galleons.*

> ....FASCINATING FACT....
> The biggest Spanish galleons weighed well
> over 1,000 tons.

169

The age of sail

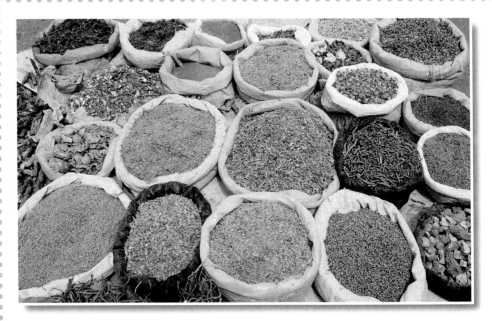

▲ *Spices are still sold in the east today just as they were hundreds of years ago.*

- **East Indiamen** were ships that carried ivory, silks, and spices to Europe from India, China, and the East Indies.

- **By 1800** Indiamen could carry 1,000 tons of cargo.

- **Packet ships** were ships that provided a regular service across the Atlantic between Europe and the U.S.A.—they sailed regardless of whether they had a full load.

- **The first packet service** began in 1818 with the Black Ball Line from Liverpool to New York. Red Star and Swallowtail followed.

- **Clippers** were the big, fast sailing ships that "clipped off" time as they raced to get cargoes of tea from China and India back first to markets in Europe and the U.S.A.

- **Clippers** had slender hulls, tall masts, and up to 35 sails.

- **Clippers could reach** speeds of 30 knots (35 mph/55 km/h). Many could sail from New York, around South America, to San Francisco in under 100 days.

- **In 1866** the clippers *Taeping*, *Serica*, and *Ariel* raced 15,970 mi (25,700 km) from Foochow in China to London in 99 days.

- **Canadian Donald Mckay** of Boston, Massachusetts, was the greatest clipper builder. His ship the *Great Republic* of 1853 was the biggest sailing ship of its time, over 330 ft (100 m) long and able to carry 4,000 tons of cargo.

- **A famous clipper,** the *Cutty Sark*, built in 1869 is preserved at Greenwich, London. Its name is Scottish for "short shirt" and comes from the witch in Robert Burns's poem "Tam O'Shanter."

▶ *The tea clippers of the mid 1800s were the pinnacle of sailing ship technology, able to carry thousands of tons of tea at speeds of 20 knots or more.*

171

A sailor's life

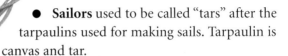

▶ *A traditional form of punishment for sailors was a whip called the cat- o'-nine-tails.*

- **Sailors** used to be called "tars" after the tarpaulins used for making sails. Tarpaulin is canvas and tar.

- **A sailor's duties** included climbing masts, rigging sails, taking turns on watch, and swabbing (cleaning) decks.

- **The eight-hour** watches were timed with an hour glass.

- **Storing food** on ships in the days before canning was a problem. Sailors survived on biscuits and dried meat.

- **Hard tack** was a hard biscuit that kept for years but often became infested with maggots. The maggots were picked out before the biscuit was eaten.

- **Every sailor** had a daily ration of water of a quart (just over a liter) since all water had to be carried on board.

- **Sailors** often made clothes from spare materials such as sail canvas.

- **Sailors who offended** against discipline might be flogged with a "cat-o'-nine-tails"—a whip with nine lengths of knotted cord.

- **Sailors slept** in any corner they could find, often next to the cannon or in the darkness below decks.

- **Sailors' lavatories** on old ships were simply holes overhanging the sea called "jardines," from the French for garden.

▲ *The introduction of the hammock in the 18th century made sleeping much less uncomfortable for sailors.*

Boat building

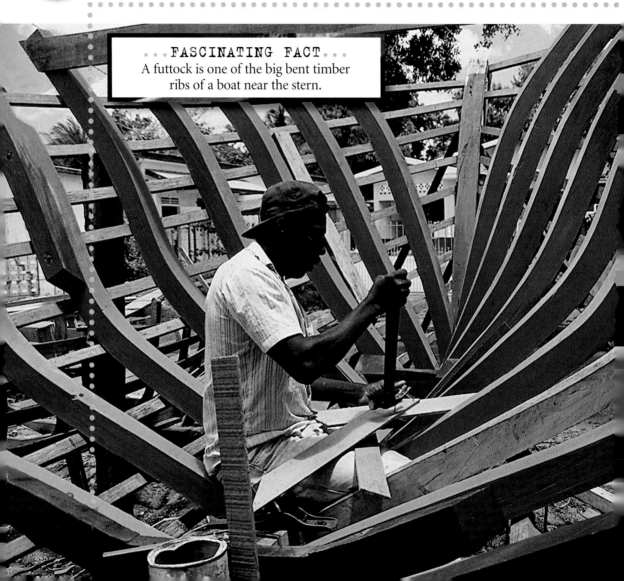

...FASCINATING FACT...
A futtock is one of the big bent timber
ribs of a boat near the stern.

- **For much of history** ships were built and designed by shipwrights.

- **Shipwrights** worked from experience and rarely drew plans. But in the 17th and 18th centuries, they often made models.

- **Nowadays** ships are designed by "naval architects" and built by shipbuilders.

- **Wooden ships** were put together on a building berth. Timbers and planks were cut and shaped around, then fitted together on the berth to form the ship's hull.

- **First the long spine** or keel of the boat was laid down. Thick wooden ribs were added to make a strong frame.

- **In the Middle Ages** in the Mediterranean, wooden ships were carvel-built. This means the planks were fitted together edge to edge onto the ribs of the structure.

- **In the Middle Ages** in northern Europe, wooden ships were clinker-built. This means the planks overlapped, as in Viking ships.

- **Ships** are launched down a slope called a slipway.

- **After launching,** a ship has just the bare bones of a hull and main structures. It is finished in a fitting-out basin.

Ocean liners

- **The great age** of ocean liners lasted from the early 1900s to the 1950s.

- **Ocean liners** were huge boats, often with luxurious cabins, bars, games rooms, and swimming pools.

- **The main route** was across the Atlantic. From 1833 liners competed for the Blue Riband title for fastest crossing.

- **Great Blue Riband** contenders included Brunel's *Great Western* in the 1830s, the *Mauretania* which held it from 1907 to 1929, and the French *Normandie* of the 1930s.

◄ *One of the great transatlantic liners of the 1930s, the* Queen Mary *(sister-ship of the* Queen Elizabeth*) is now a hotel at Long Beach, California.*

▲ *The* Grand Princess *is the world's second largest passenger ship, with rooms for 2,600 people.*

- **The last ocean liner** to hold the Blue Riband was the *United States* in the 1960s.

- **The famous Cunard line** was set up by Nova Scotia Quaker Samuel Cunard with George Burns and David MacIver in 1839.

- **The *Titanic*** was the largest ship ever built at 46,329 tons when launched in 1912, but it sank on its maiden (first) voyage.

- **The sinking** of the liner *Lusitania* by a German submarine on May 7, 1915 with the loss of 1,198 lives spurred the U.S. to join the war against Germany.

- **The *Queen Elizabeth*,** launched in 1938, was the largest passenger ship ever built—1,030 ft (314 m) long and 83,673 tons. It burned and sank during refitting in Hong Kong in 1972.

- **Future liners** may be based on FastShip technology, with a very broad flat hull for high-speed stability.

Submersibles

- **Submersibles** are small underwater craft. Some are designed for very deep descents for ocean research. Others are designed for exploring wrecks.

- **One early submersible** was a strong metal ball or bathysphere, lowered by cables from a ship.

- **The bathysphere** was built by Americans William Beebe and Otis Barton who went down 2,900 ft (900 m) in it off Bermuda on June 11, 1931. The possibility of the cable snapping meant the bathysphere was very dangerous.

- **The bathyscaphe** could be controlled underwater, unlike the bathysphere. Its strong steel hull meant it could descend 13,123 ft (4,000 m).

- **The first bathyscaphe**, the *FNRS 2*, was developed by Swiss scientist August Piccard between 1946 and 1948. An improved version, the *FNRS 3*, descended 13,123 ft (4,000 m) off Senegal on February 15, 1954.

- **In the 1960s** the Woods Hole Oceanographic Institute in the U.S.A. began to develop a smaller, more maneuverable submersible, called *Alvin*.

- **ROVs** or Remote Operated Vehicles are small robot submersibles. ROVs are controlled from a ship with video cameras and computer virtual reality systems. Using the ROV *Argo-Jason*, Robert Ballard found the wreck of the liner *Titanic* in 1985.

  > **...FASCINATING FACT...**
  > On January 23, 1960, the bathyscaphe *Trieste*, controlled by August Piccard's son Jacques, descended a record 35,814 ft in the Marianas Trench in the Pacific.

- *Deep Flight* is a revolutionary submersible with wings that can fly underwater like an airplane, turning, diving, banking, and rolling.

- **A new breed** of small submersibles, like the *Sea Star* and *Deep Rover*, cost about the same as a big car and are designed for sports as well as research.

▼ *This is one of the first of the huge range of submersibles that began to appear in the 1960s and 70s. They are now much smaller and more maneuverable, but still work in much the same way.*

Double hatch containing airlock for divers to go out

Propeller for pushing the craft through the water

Powerful electric motor

Cabin of strong steel to resist intense water pressure

Entry hatch

Searchlights for seeing the dark ocean depths

Batteries

To go back up to the surface, the pilot switches off the electromagnets that hold the ballast of iron balls in place

Float filled with gasoline. Since gasoline is lighter than water, it helps keep the craft afloat

Video camera

Claw for grabbing samples

Extra strong perspex dome

As the craft descends, the gasoline is compressed and gives less buoyancy, speeding the descent

179

Submarines

▲ *Nuclear submarines can stay submerged for months at a time.*

- **The first workable submarine** was a rowing boat covered with waterproofed skins, built by Dutch scientist Cornelius Van Drebbel in 1620.

- **In 1776** David Bushnell's one-man submarine, the *Turtle*, attacked British ships in America's War of Independence.

- **Gasoline engines** and electric batteries were combined to make the first successful subs in the 1890s.

- **Powerful**, less polluting diesel engines took over from 1908.

- **In 1954** the U.S.A. launched the *Nautilus*, the first nuclear powered sub. Now all subs are nuclear-powered.

- **U-boats** were German subs that attack Allied convoys of ships in World Wars I and II.

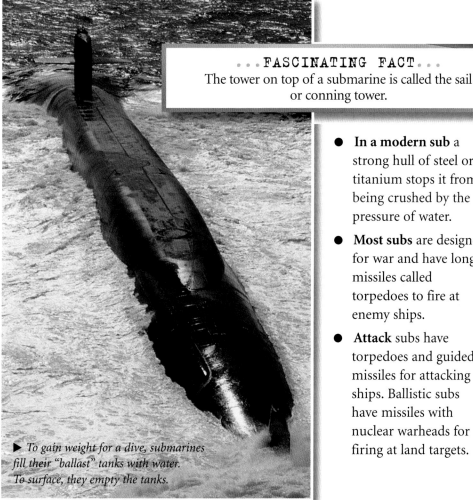

▶ *To gain weight for a dive, submarines fill their "ballast" tanks with water. To surface, they empty the tanks.*

...FASCINATING FACT...
The tower on top of a submarine is called the sail or conning tower.

● **In a modern sub** a strong hull of steel or titanium stops it from being crushed by the pressure of water.

● **Most subs** are designed for war and have long missiles called torpedoes to fire at enemy ships.

● **Attack** subs have torpedoes and guided missiles for attacking ships. Ballistic subs have missiles with nuclear warheads for firing at land targets.

Warships

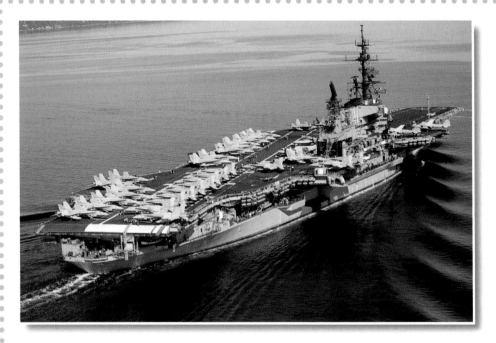

▲ *The mightiest warships of the modern era are the U.S. navy's nuclear-powered aircraft carriers.*

- **21st-century navies** have five main classes of surface warship in descending size order: aircraft carriers, assault ships, cruisers, destroyers, and frigates.

- **The biggest** warships are 1,092 ft- (332.9 m-) long U.S. aircraft carriers *Nimitz, Dwight D. Eisenhower, Carl Vinson, Abraham Lincoln, John C. Stennis, George Washington,* and *Harry S. Truman.*

- **In World War II** cruisers had big guns and often acted independently; destroyers protected the main fleet; and frigates protected slower ships against submarines.

182

- **The distinction between** classes is now blurred. Cruisers are rare, and many small warships carry helicopters or even VTOL planes (see warplanes).

- **The Russian** Moskva class are a cross between cruisers and aircraft carriers with rear flight decks for helicopters.

- **The British** Invincible class are small aircraft carriers able to carry six Harrier jump jets and twelve helicopters.

- **Warships** have largely replaced guns with guided missiles.

- **Warships** have both short-range missiles to fire against missiles and long-range supersonic missiles to fire against ships up to 300 mi (500 km) away.

- **The U.S. Ticonderoga** ships are small cruisers built in the 1970s. They are powered by gas-turbine engines and armed with Tomahawk nuclear or conventional missiles.

- **The nuclear-powered** Russian Kirov class begun in 1973 are among the few big cruisers, over 22,000 tons.

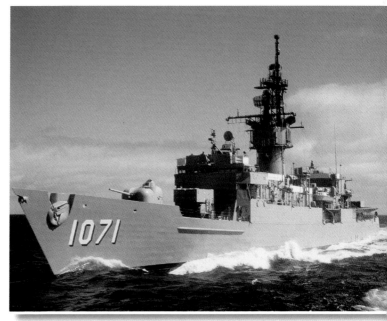

▶ *A 1940s destroyer armed with a rotating gun for fleet escort.*

Hovercraft

- **A hovercraft** or air cushion vehicle floats on a layer of compressed air just above the ground. It is also called a ground-effect machine. The air means there is very little friction between the craft and the ground.

- **A hovercraft** has one or more big fans that suck air into the craft, then blow it down underneath. The air is trapped underneath by a flexible rubber skirt.

▼ *Hovercraft vary in speed, size, and power, but they are used essentially for one of two purposes: as ferries across short stretches of water, like this one, or by the army and navy.*

Flight deck

Passenger compartment in which people travel as they would on an airplane. There is no deck as on a conventional boat

Rudders to steer the craft. These become more effective the faster the hovercraft is traveling

Rubberized bag skirt, holding the air cushion in

Powerful gas turbine for the lifting fan

Double propellers for driving the hovercraft forward or backward at speeds of up to 72 mph (120 km/h)

- **The idea began with** Sir John Thornycroft in the 1870s. He thought drag on a ship's hull could be reduced if an indent allowed it to ride on a cushion of air. But no-one could figure out how to contain the air.

> **...FASCINATING FACT...**
> Hospitals may use special hoverbeds to support badly burned patients on air.

- **In the 1950s** Christopher Cockerell cracked the problem by pumping air down around the edge of a curtain-like skirt. The air itself then sealed the cushion of air inside the curtain.

- **In 1959** the world's first practical hovercraft, the *SRN1*, was built using Cockerell's system. It crossed the English Channel on the 50th anniversary of Blériot's first flight across the Channel.

- **In the late 1960s** the U.S. army and navy began using hovercraft in the Vietnam War for patrol and rescue missions because of their ability to go over land, water, and swampy ground equally easily. The Russian and U.S. armies are still the biggest users of hovercraft.

- **In 1968** big hovercraft able to carry scores of cars and trucks were introduced as ferries across the English Channel, but elsewhere they have not lived up to expectations. The biggest cross-Channel hovercraft was the 185 ft- (56 m-) long *SRN4 MkIII* which carried 418 passengers and 60 cars.

- **In the late 1950s,** French engineer Jean Bertin developed a train called a tracked air cushion vehicle. This is like a hovercraft on rails. Trains like this could swish between cities almost silently at speeds of 300 mph (500 km/h).

- **On January 25, 1980** a 100 ton U.S. Navy hovercraft, the *SES 100-B*, reached a record speed of 105.6 mph (170 km/h)—faster than any warship has ever traveled.

Hydrofoils

- **Hydrofoils** are boats with hulls that lift up above the water when traveling at high speeds.

- **The hydrofoils** are wings attached to the hull by struts that move underwater like airplane wings and lift the boat up.

- **Because only the foils** dip in the water, hydrofoils avoid water resistance, so can travel faster with less power.

- **Surface-piercing hydrofoils** are used in calm inland waters and skim across the surface.

- **Fully-submerged hydrofoils** dip deep into the water for stability in seagoing boats.

▲ *Surface-piercing hydrofoil*   ▲ *Fully-submerged hydrofoil*

▲ *By lifting themselves out of the water and almost flying across the surface, hydrofoils achieve very high speeds.*

- **The foils** are usually in two sets: bow and stern.

- **The bow and stern foils** are in one of three arrangements. "Canard" means the stern foil is bigger. "Airplane" means the bow foil is bigger. "Tandem" means they are both the same size.

- **The first successful hydrofoil** was built by Italian Enrico Forlanini in 1906.

- **In 1918** Alexander Graham Bell, inventor of the telephone, built a hydrofoil that set a world water speed record at 61.6 knots (70.8 mph/114 km/h). The record was not beaten until the American *Fresh 1*, another hydrofoil, set a new record of 84 knots (96.9 mph/155 km/h) in 1963.

...FASCINATING FACT...
The biggest hydrofoil is the 210 ft long, 50 knots (57 mph) *Plainview* navy ship.

Canoes

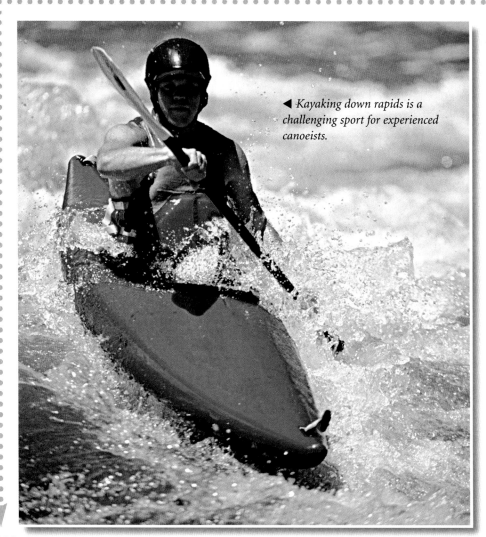

◀ *Kayaking down rapids is a challenging sport for experienced canoeists.*

- **The first canoes** were scooped-out logs.

- **A skin canoe** was made by stretching animal skins over a bent wood frame.

- **A skin canoe** dating from around 4500BC has been discovered on the Baltic island of Fünen.

- **Some skin canoes** are round like the Indian paracil and the Welsh coracle.

- **Some skin canoes** are long and thin like the Irish curach and the Inuit kayak.

- **Kayaks** have a watertight cover made from sealskin to keep out water in rough conditions.

- **The ancient quffa** of Iraq is a large canoe made of basketwork sealed with tar and dates back to 4000BC.

- **Native Americans** made canoes from bark. The Algonquins used paper birch, the Iroquois elm.

- **Bark canoes** were the basis for today's sport canoes of fiberglass, plastic, and aluminum.

- **Unlike ordinary boats** canoes are often so light that they can easily be carried overland to avoid waterfalls or to move from one river to another.

▼ *The materials may be different, but today's bright fiberglass canoes are based on the same principles as the ancient bark canoes of Native Americans.*

189

Great voyages

- **In 330BC** the Greek sailor Pytheas sailed out into the Atlantic through the Straits of Gibraltar and found his way to "Thule" (Britain).

- **Around AD1000** the Viking Leif Ericsson was the first European to cross the Atlantic to North America.

▲ *Francis Drake was the first Englishman to sail around the world in 1580.*

- **In 1405** Chinese admiral Cheng Ho began a series of seven epic voyages around the Indian Ocean in a huge fleet of junks.

- **In 1492** Genoese Christopher Columbus crossed the Atlantic from Cadiz in Spain and discovered the New World. His ship was the *Santa Maria*.

- **From 1499 to 1504** Italian Amerigo Vespucci sailed the Atlantic and realized South America was a continent. America is named after him.

- **In 1492** Italian John Cabot crossed the North Atlantic from Bristol in England and found Canada.

- **In 1498** Portuguese Vasco da Gama was the first European to reach India by sea, sailing all around Africa.

- **In 1642** Dutchman Abel Tasman sailed to what is now Australia and New Zealand. The island of Tasmania is named after him.

- **From 1768 to 79** James Cook explored the South Pacific in his ship the *Endeavour* and landed at Botany Bay.

▶ *Between 1492 and 1504 Colombus explored the West Indies and the coasts of Central and South America.*

▼ *Captain Cook reached Australia in his ship the* Endeavour.

.·**FASCINATING FACT**·.
In 1522, Ferdinand Magellan's ship *Victoria* made the first round-the-world voyage.

191

Docks and ports

- **Some ports,** like Hong Kong and Rio, are based on natural harbors; others are constructed artificially.

- **The Phoenicians** built artificial harbors at Tyre and Sidon in the Lebanon in the 13th century.

- **The Romans** invented waterproof concrete to build the quays and breakwaters at their port of Ostia.

- **Roman and other ancient ports** had animal and human powered cranes. Saxon London and Viking Dublin had well-built wooden wharves.

- **Traditionally**, big boats would anchor in mid stream and barges called lighters would take the cargo ashore.

▼ *The port of Balstad in Norway, a perfect natural harbor.*

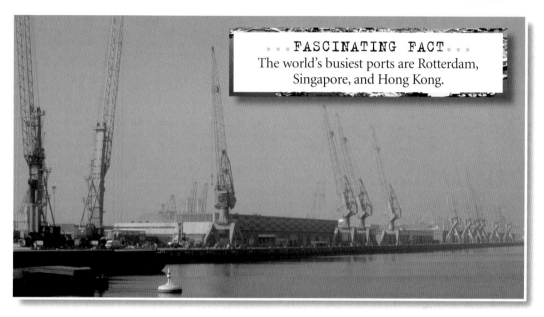

▲ *The Dutch port of Rotterdam is the largest in the world.*

- **In the 18th century** the first enclosed deep-water docks were built at London and Liverpool. Here it was possible for big ships to moor and unload directly onto the wharves.

- **In the 20th century**, ports specializing in particular cargoes, such as oil terminals, grew.

- **Since the 1950s** there has been a huge growth in container ports. Containers are big standardized metal crates that can be unloaded quickly.

- **The world's main container ports** are Hong Kong, Singapore, Rotterdam, Hamburg, and New York.

Rescue boats

- **Several designs** for "unsinkable" lifeboats were tried in 18th-century France and England.

- **After many people drowned** when the ship *Adventure* went down in 1789, a contest for a lifeboat was set up.

- **The contest winner** was Newcastle boatbuilder Henry Greathead. His boat the *Original* would right itself when capsized and still float even when nearly filled with water.

- **The first land-based** powered lifeboat was steam-powered and launched in 1890.

- **Around 1907** diesel-power lifeboats were introduced. Without the need for oars, most of the boat could be covered in and so made even more unsinkable.

▲ *This is a typical inflatable inshore rescue boat. Boats like these are bonded together by heat and glue, and are incredibly tough.*

- **Modern land-based lifeboats** are either steel-hulled or made of a double-skin of timber.

- **The hull** usually contains a large number of sealed air containers so it is almost impossible for the boat to sink.

- **Some lifeboats** are afloat all the time. Others are kept ashore in a lifeboat house ready for emergencies.

- **Lifeboats** kept ashore are launched down a slipway into the ocean or wheeled into the ocean on a cradle until they float.

- **As leisure sailing** and swimming has increased, so there has been an increase in the number of inshore rescue boats. These are small rubber or fiberglass boats, kept afloat by an inflatable tube of toughened rubber.

▲ *Offshore lifeboats can be lauched down a slipway. This allows them to hit the water at speed and reach the scene of an emergency as quickly as possible.*

Sailing and tacking

- **Sailing ships** can sail into the wind because the wind does not so much push the sail as suck it.

- **The sail** is always angled so that the wind blows across it, allowing it to act like the wing of an aircraft.

- **As the wind blows** over the curve of the sail, it speeds up and its pressure drops in front of the sail. The extra pressure gained from the other side drives the boat forward.

- **The sail** works as long as the wind is blowing straight across it, so to go in a particular direction, the sailor simply changes the angle of the sail.

- **The boat's keel** or centerboard stops it from slipping sideways.

▼ *The record speed reached by a sailing vessel was 53.4 mph (86 km/h) on a 1,640 ft (500 m) run.*

- **The boat can sail** with the wind behind it, to the side of it, or even slightly ahead of it.

- **To sail directly** or nearly directly into the wind, a boat has to "tack." This means zig-zagging back and forth across the path of the wind so wind is always blowing across the sails.

- **At the end** of each tack, the sail "comes about" (changes course). The tiller (steering arm) is turned to point the boat on the new course and the sail is allowed to "gibe" (swing over to the other side).

- **Sailing close to the wind** is sailing nearly into the wind.

- **Running with the wind** is sailing with a fast wind behind.

▶ *With their sails in line with the hull, these yachts are sailing close to the wind.*

First steamships

◄ *Steam-driven warships like this were built in the 1880s.*

- **In 1783** French nobleman Marquis Claude de Jouffroy d'Abbans built a huge steam boat that churned up the Saone River near Lyon in France for 15 minutes before the pounding engines shook it to pieces.

- **In 1787** American John Fitch made the first successful steamship with an engine driving a series of paddles.

- **In 1790** Fitch started the world's first steam service on the Delaware River.

- **In 1802** Scot William Symington built a tug, the *Charlotte Dundas*, able to tow two 70-ton barges.

- **In 1807** American Robert Fulton made the first passenger steam boats, running 150 mi (240 km) up the Hudson River from New York.

- **In 1819** the New York-built ship *Savannah* made the first steam-assisted crossing of the Atlantic.

- **In 1833** Canadian ship *Royal William* made the first mainly steam-powered Atlantic crossing in two days.

- **In 1843** British engineer Isambard Kingdom Brunel launched the first all-iron hull steamship, the *Great Britain*.

- **In 1858** Brunel launched *Great Eastern*, the biggest ship of the 19th century, 692 ft (211 m) long and weighing 30,000 tons.

- **Early steamships** had paddles, but in 1835 Swede John Ericsson invented a screw propeller. In 1845 a screw-driven boat won a tug-of-war with a paddle steamer.

▶ *A Mississippi paddle steamer.*

Yachts and catamarans

- **The word yacht** comes from the 17th-century Dutch word jacht, which meant "ship for chasing."

- **English yachting** began in 1662 when King Charles II raced his brother James on the Thames for a £100 bet in a small pleasure boat given to him by the Dutch.

- **In 1898** Joshua Slocum sailed single-handed round the world in the 37 ft (11.3 m) *Spray*, proving the sea-worthiness of small craft.

- **From the 1920s** the same aerodynamic principles applied to hulls were used for sails and rigging.

- **Most racing yachts** are now built from aluminum and light, strong composites such as carbon-fiber.

- **In the 1960s** twin-hulled catamarans became popular since they pierce waves well yet are wide and stable.

▶ *Yachting is now a popular pastime and professional sport. Numerous tournaments are held throughout the world.*

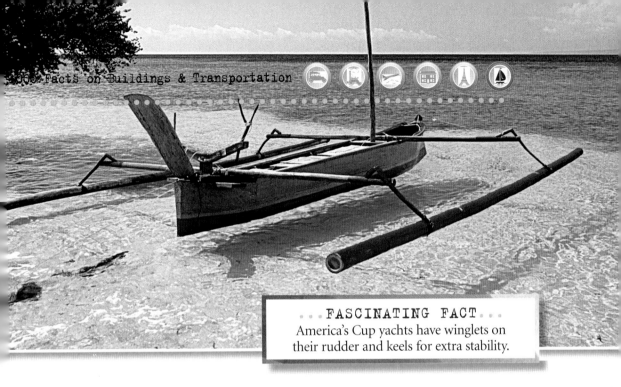

▲ *Made of lightweight materials, catamarans have two shallow hulls which allow them to slip through the water with little resistance. Catamarans with twin hulls and outriggers (extra floats) are all developed from traditional Polynesian outriggers.*

- **In 1983** Australian Ben Lexcen became the first non-American to win the famous America's Cup race.

- **The key to Lexcen's** success was revolutionary winglets on the keel to improve stability.

- **Sails on some yachts** are now computer-controlled to keep them at exactly the right angle.

Powerboats

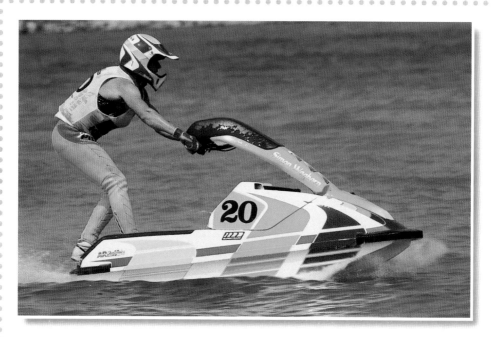

▲ *The engine of a jet ski sucks in water and pumps it out of the back pushing the ski forward.*

- **Powerboating** began in 1863 when Frenchman Jean Lenoir installed a gasoline engine in a small boat.

- **The first major race** was in 1903 across the English Channel. The Gold Cup, organized by the American Power Boat Association (APBA), started on the Hudson in 1904.

- **In about 1910** motor makers like Evinrude introduced detachable "outboard" motors that clamp to the stern. Inboard motors have the engine built into the hull.

- **In the 1920s** racing boats adopted "planing hulls" for skimming across the water at high speeds, rather than traditional deep v-shaped "displacement" hulls. After World War II hulls were made more and more, not from wood, but metals and fiberglass.

- **Most powerboats** are driven by a high-speed jet of water as opposed to by a propeller screw.

- **In 1994** American Tom Gentry set the offshore Class 1 record of 157.4 mph (253.35 km/h) in Skater powerboats.

- **In 1996** Gentry's *Gentry Eagle* crossed the Atlantic in 2 days 14 hours 7 mins. In 1997, the skipper *Destriero* made it in 2 days 6 hours 34 minutes.

- **The official water speed** record is 317.58 mph (511.11 km/h) by Kenneth Warby in his hydroplane *Spirit of Australia* on Blowering Lake, New South Wales on October 8, 1978.

- **Jet skis** are like motorboats that skim across the water on a ski. They were developed by the American Clayton Jacobsen back in the 1960s.

- **The jet ski** speed record is 43 mph (69 km/h) by French D. Condemine in 1994 on a Yahama.

▲ *Powerboat racing has become hugely competitive like motor racing, and Formula One boats roar around at speeds over 125 mph (200 km/h).*

Canals

▲ *The Suez Canal opened in 1869 and shortened the route between England and India by 6,000 mi (15,500 ␣*

- **In 1470BC** the Egyptian Pharaoh Sesostris had the first Suez Canal built, linking the Mediterranean and Red Sea.

- **The Grand Canal** in China is the world's longest man-made waterway, running 1,085 mi (1,747 km) west of Beijing.

- **The origins** of the Grand Canal date to the 4th century BC, but it was rebuilt in AD607.

- **The late 1700s and early 1800s** saw many canals built for the factories of the Industrial Revolution, like the Bridgwater Canal in Lancashire, England.

- **Clinton's Folly** is the Erie Canal linking Lake Erie to the Hudson, pushed through by governor De Witt Clinton in 1825.

- **The current Suez Canal** was built by Ferdinand de Lesseps (1859–1869). It is the world's longest big-ship canal, 100.59 mi (161.9 km) long.

- **The Panama Canal** links the Atlantic and Pacific Oceans 50.9 mi (82 km) across Central America, cutting the ocean voyage from New York to San Francisco by 8,948 mi (14,400 km).

- **The Panama Canal** takes over 400 million tons of shipping a year.

- **The world's busiest canal** is Germany's Kiel which takes 45,000 ships a year from the North Sea to the Baltic.

- **In Russia** one of the world's longest canal systems links the Black Sea to the Arctic Ocean via the Volga River.

▲ *Amsterdam's canals were dug in the city's heyday in the 1600s.*

205

Navigation

- **Early sailors** found their way by staying near land, looking for "landmarks" on shore. Away from land they steered by stars, so had only a vague idea of direction in the day.

- **After c.1100** European sailors used a magnetic compass needle to find North.

- **A compass** only gives you a direction to steer; it does not tell you where you are.

- **The astrolabe** was used from c.1350. This measured the angle of a star above the horizon, or the Sun at noon and so gave a rough idea of latitude (how far north or south of the Equator).

GPS satellite

GPS receiver

20.96 ' E

48.18 ' N

Satellites orbit in six groups of four each

▲▶ *In the the Global Positioning System, sometimes known as "satellite navigation," 24 satellites in orbit around the Earth send out radio signals to the surface. At any place on the planet, signals from at least three satellites can be detected and compared by a hand-held receiver, to fix a location within 30 to 165 ft (10 to 50 m).*

- **From the 1500s** the cross-staff gave a more accurate measure of latitude at night from the angle between the Pole Star and the horizon.

- **From the mid-1700s** until the 1950s, sailors measured latitude with a mirror sextant. This had two mirrors. It gave the angle of a star (or the Sun) when one mirror was adjusted until the star was at horizon height in the other.

- **For centuries** the only way to find longitude—how far east or west—was by dead reckoning. This meant trailing a knotted rope in the water to keep track of speed, and so estimate how far you had come.

- **You can find longitude** by comparing the Sun's height with its height at the same time at a longitude you know. But early pendulum clocks did not work well enough aboard ship to give the correct time.

- **The longitude problem** was solved in the 1700s when John Harrison made a very accurate spring-driven clock or chronometer.

- **Ships** can now find their position with pinpoint accuracy using the Global Positioning System or GPS. This works by electronically comparing signals from a ring of satellites.

▶ *A navigational instrument for measuring latitude from the angle of certain stars.*

207

Index

Index

Index

Index

Index

Index

Index

Index

Acknowledgments

The publishers would like to thank the following artists who have contributed to this book:

Nicholas Forder, Janos Marffy, Terry Riley, Peter Sarson, Mike White

The publishers would like to thank the following sources for the use of their photographs:

Page 40 CORBIS ; Page 49 Joseph Sohm ChromoSohm Inc/CORBIS; Page 52 Wolfgang Kaehler/CORBIS; Page 73 CORBIS; Page 79 Yann Arthus-Betrand/CORBIS; Page 165 Eye Ubiquitous/CORBIS

All other pictures from the Miles Kelly Archives.